The Secret Bristol Downs

GERALDINE TAYLOR

with drawings
by
SUSANNA KENDALL

REDCLIFFE
Bristol

First published in 1992 by
Redcliffe Press Ltd
49 Park St, Bristol.

ISBN 1 872971 82 2

British Cataloguing-in-Publication Data.
A catalogue record for this book is
available from the British Library.

Typeset and printed by
The Longdunn Press Ltd., Bristol.

CONTENTS

THE BRISTOL DOWNS

I became the Downs Ranger in 1976. Since then I have had plenty of surprises, including the sight of a lizard sunning itself on a rock and an encounter with a doe red deer running across Ladies Mile.

On the Downs, every season has its highlights and its special atmosphere.

Spring is a time of excitement – plants are emerging with bright new growth, trees are bursting into life, nesting birds are busy in the undergrowth and the air is filled with the scent of blossom.

In early summer, the wildlife seems to settle into a routine and enjoy itself – especially the newly-fledged birds. Late summer, by contrast, with its dark and dusty foliage, is almost a sad time. This is when I look forward to the autumn when the leaves change colour, fall and make a golden carpet.

Early winter is a particularly good time to start spotting birds as it is now possible to see between the trees and through the undergrowth.

Life seems to stop after Christmas and on the surface everything appears dull – but the first signs of spring are there already if you know where to look.

As you read this book, you too will discover the excitement in a year of life on the Bristol Downs.

Gordon Milward
Downs Ranger

We are extremely fortunate in Bristol to have such an area of open parkland as the Downs. It is in a unique position both in its proximity to the city centre, and in its setting beside the Avon Gorge.

It was decreed in the Clifton & Durdham Downs (Bristol) Act of 1861 that the Downs 'shall forever thereafter be kept open and unenclosed and a place for the public resort and recreation of the citizens and inhabitants of Bristol.' It is comforting to know that, other than by Act of Parliament, this wonderful area is safe from development for all future time.

We are in this fortunate position because of the foresight and generosity of the Society of Merchant Venturers. When

Durdham Down was offered for sale in the middle of the nineteenth century, they persuaded the City Fathers to purchase it. To encourage them to do this the Society offered to include Clifton Down to come within the 1861 Downs Act, enabling the whole Downs to be retained as an open space in perpetuity.

The Downs are a haven for wildlife. Careful tree planting and conservation of natural areas have encouraged this, and we are indebted to the work of the Downs Ranger and all those involved with its maintenance. The Downs are a source of great interest and pleasure to many and are particularly beneficial to the children of our city who are able to experience wildlife at first hand. I commend this book to you, which illustrates the variety of wildlife that can be found on the Downs in its natural habitat.

Alan Tasker
Merchant Venturer

INTRODUCTION

Until the end of the eighteenth century Clifton and Durdham Downs were vast remote heathlands, golden with gorse, chin-deep in bracken and grazed by thousands of sheep. In 1754, a Mr Owen referred to the Downs as lonely wastelands, 'covered with fern and furze', above cliffs 'rough, craggy and romantick beyond imagination'. There was an abundance of wildlife, and during the reign of Elizabeth I (1558–1603), the Avon Gorge was famous for its falcons. Other early recorded birdlife included linnets, larks, warblers and nightingales.

However, in 1611 and 1712 the owners of Durdham Down, the Lords of Henbury, granted mining licences for Durdham Down which were to have a profound effect on the wild heaths of the Downs. At the beginning of the eighteenth century Durdham Down alone comprised 2,000 acres but, as a result of mining operations and building encroachments, by 1860 this had been reduced to 212 acres.

In 1676 the Society of Merchant Venturers purchased the 230 acres of Clifton Down from the Manor of Clifton and then in 1860, nearly two centuries later, the City of Bristol bought Durdham Down. The following year the Downs were secured by an Act of Parliament to remain as open spaces for the use of the citizens of Bristol. The Bristol Downs thus became the 442 acres we have today.

The popularity of the Downs as a recreational area increased rapidly, with inevitable consequences for the plant-life. In his *The Bristol Flora* (1912), the botanist J.W. White explains,

> The golden gorse-covered and heathy commons of our fathers have completely vanished under the trampling of growing crowds. Many of the smaller hawthorns and hollies are being destroyed without hope of replacement, for no seedling or sapling has the remotest chance of raising its head under the hoofs of the gallopers; and wide stretches of bare turf have ceased to show any sign of the characteristic vegetation with which the Downs at one time abounded. At the present day those interesting plants must be looked for on rocky ledges, screes, and slopes for which the golfer and footballer have no use.

Averil Morley, writing in 1934 of the bird-life of the Bristol Downs, also commented on public ignorance of the Downs:

> Most people imagine the bird-life of the Downs to consist of a few sparrows; one or two pairs of long-suffering blackbirds

> and thrushes; perhaps a wren and a hedgesparrow in the remotest parts.

Her text evinces both the extraordinarily rich bird-life of the Bristol Downs (recorded birds include hawfinch, little owl, tawny owl, spotted flycatcher and yellowhammer) and the power of the Downs to inspire wildlife observers to poetry in their narratives. Here, Averil Morley describes May bird-song in Black Rock Gully.

> Below in the crowded valley, the lovely, lazy contralto of the blackbirds is a contrast to the energetic and ringing peals of the thrushes; while the slow trickling song of the robins is different again from the sweet impetuosity of the wrens; the clear pure jingling of greenfinches; the musical scramble of whitethroats; the simple notes of chiffchaffs; the languid ramblings of garden-warblers; the marsh tit singing like a peal of bells; the well-beloved notes of the cuckoo; and, this from the darkest, most sunless depths of the Gully, the dionysian song of the blackcap – all this wonderful pattern of music woven on to the refrains of willow-warblers and chaffinches, the two commonest birds at this time of the year, surpasses in quantity and quality any other chorus of birds of which I know. One hardly misses the vanished nightingales.

Imagining this richness, it is jolting to read a contemporary assessment of the wildlife situation on the Downs. Writing in 1987 for the Bristol Naturalists' Society publication *The Avon Gorge* S.D. Micklewright comments,

> The Downs were once a superb wildlife haven providing homes for typical downland plants and birds, but they are increasingly managed in the style of a municipal park with little attention paid to wildlife requirements.

All is not lost. Mr Micklewright explains how wildlife and recreational interests can co-exist on the Downs and this is slowly – if precariously – being achieved. Once again the wildlife of the Downs is experiencing a time of change. This time, the change is for the better.

Large areas of the Downs have been left unmown and many meadow plants believed diminished or lost have appeared. Orchids are increasing and in 1992 the nationally scarce green-winged orchid appeared for the first time. Once again, peregrine falcons rule the Avon Gorge.

I have looked into the records of the past to tell me about wildlife gone by and I expect that in an hundred years from now, researchers will use this book in the same way.

I hope that their reaction will not be sadness at what has been lost to the Downs in those hundred years but surprise at what more has been gained since this was written. What is a nature wonderland in 1992 could, in 2092, be a paradise for wildlife and for Bristol.

Geraldine Taylor

Note

No two years are alike on the Downs. This is fascinating for the observer but frustrating for anyone attempting to see a flower in bloom on exactly the same day as that recorded by a diarist. Allow a week or two either way, especially if the spring is exceptionally early or late.

Birds and animals are often more active in the early morning and I've acknowledged this by recording the time at which some of my observations were made.

JANUARY

1ST The mistle thrush is shouting from the beech this afternoon and redwings are assembling in groups and flying nervously from hawthorn bushes to the lower horse chestnut branches and back again. Two fieldfares fly among them.

'Sticky buds' on the chestnuts are fat and tacky, but the ash buds are black and prim, promising nothing.

An early patch of blue sweet violets has three flowers and 31 buds; the leaves of the plant smell as sweetly as the flowers.

7TH 7.30 a.m. The muddy turf of the football pitches is full of earthworms mating: a grotesque, pink performance.

The buds of the wayfaring tree are like miniature Viking helmets.

14TH Last night's gales have blown the dead leaves away from this copse and bright green loops of dog's mercury are emerging in the exposed earth. Some of the plants have already raised their heads of neatly pleated leaves above the ground.

A trio of earthstars beside a path in Fairyland! Perfectly named, these are the most elusive and romantic of fungi.

Earthstars

20TH Hundreds of redwings on the Granny Downs are turning over the brown leaves they so closely resemble.

Two rooks face each other by the Seven Sisters: the tips of their beaks are touching like a mirror image.

On the edge of the Gorge, the clumps and spires of the gorse are a rich golden-yellow; at least three pairs of bullfinches are hiding there.

The green woodpecker is fluffed up against the cold and pecking furiously at the grass.

22**ND** The great tits are the loudest singers this morning – I walk a quarter of a mile away from one and can still hear its repetitive calling.

There's a great spotted woodpecker pecking gently at the trunk of an ash and the red rump of the bird is clearly visible against the grey bark.

29**TH 6.45 a.m.** What's this? It's a fox. I stand still. He stands still. Then he runs a few yards, stops and turns to look back at me; runs again, stops, turns to look. He completes a circle around me before he ambles off towards the city, taking his time.

I'm often asked which birds are flying in the dark of the early morning in January. It's never really black because the street lamps give light for a long way (the daisies around these lamps are wide awake all night, incidentally). Herring gulls fly in dim light, following the river – and so do crows. But darkness makes blackbirds nervous; they wait on the ground close to hedges and seats. Wood-pigeons sit like stone on the higher tree branches – the last birds to come to life in the dawn.

Sometimes, as I look at the little green lights on the lighthouses lining the Gorge, I hear an owl hoot from Leigh Woods, across the river.

THE SWEET VIOLET

Choosing the violet to represent January is a tribute to the large patch of sweet violets nearly opposite Bristol Zoo which flowers every January and sometimes even on New Year's Day itself.

From the beginning of December the sweet violet leaves smell deliciously and from this time, too, it's possible to follow the progress of the buds and watch the tiny knots become green buds standing proud. After a week or so, the green buds flush with blue and then the long-awaited day arrives when some of the flowers open and the violet petals are contrasted with vivid orange anthers.

These early sweet violets are a rich inky-violet colour – intensified by the shadiness of their setting and the heavy grey of the winter skies.

Sweet violets are the only violet to have scented flowers and, tantalisingly, the perfume seems to vanish as soon as it is enjoyed. The presence of the substance ionine in the scent dulls the sense of smell, but fortunately not for long.

By mid-March, sweet violets are flowering elsewhere on the Downs – look in shady places, under hawthorns, in the wooded areas around the Circular Road and in hollows on the Dumps. White sweet violets are more common than blue on the Downs and some believe they are even more strongly scented.

Worth searching for are the sweet violets with a subtle mixture of both colours or those white flowers with broad, pyjama-like violet stripes.

FEBRUARY

7TH **7.30 a.m.** Dawn: frost and a pale blue sky. Strange that the blackbird isn't singing from the copper beech – he's a creature of habit and was singing so loudly yesterday that I could hear him for half a mile. But the robins are singing and the mistle thrush is shouting again and I've noticed that blackbirds rarely sing in competition with them.

The moon is still shining on one side of the sky, the sun is rising blood-red on the other and the gulls are tinted pink as they fly towards it.

What are these? Two delicate yellow finches swaying on the laburnum tree among the chestnuts. Siskins! Surely a long way from their usual pine forests.

The sweet violets are stiff with frost: they look like sugar-coated sweets.

8TH **9.00 a.m.** I count 263 redwings on the Granny Downs.

10TH There are masses of mimosa-like yellow flowers on this yew, and next to it the twigs of the blackthorn are covered in promising little coral clusters.

So far, I have passed 18 pairs of blackbirds in the wooded areas around the Circular Road and none of them have been alarmed by my fairly close observation.

18TH This afternoon I find barren strawberry flowering under the blackthorn hedge. I have to look twice to see if the glistening is a flower or a raindrop. Barren strawberry manages to cup the dew and the rain longer than other flowers.

19TH **7.45 a.m.** Wild clematis is twining round the blackthorn branches and offering new, candle-like leaves.

Two pairs of bullfinches perch silently in the ash above Black Rock Gully, the salmon-pink chests of the males astonishing in the early morning sun. One flies away and a female follows immediately, keeping a respectful distance.

I watch a white feather drift down into the Gully. Suddenly a long-tailed tit darts from the bushes and catches the feather in mid-flight.

The low walls of Wills Hall are lined with cuckoo pint leaves – there's a good selection of plain and spotted leaves.

A crow is chasing a sparrowhawk around the Seven Sisters.

20TH When I can no longer hear the mistle thrush opposite the Zoo, I can hear another in Fairyland and when I am too far away to hear this one, I can hear the song of a mistle thrush in Black Rock Gully.

There are hundreds of redwings on the turf opposite the Water Tower and 44 pied wagtails on the Granny Downs near the White Tree roundabout.

26TH The leaves of just one horse chestnut have emerged from the 'sticky buds'. They look startlingly green against the dark wood of the trunk.

By the Seven Sisters, a rook is trying to take off with a half-eaten corn on the cob in its beak.

The redwings are roosting near Wills Hall in a beech tree which looks as though it's full of leaves again.

I find the first celandine bud on a sheltered bank near Fairyland.

28TH It's the end of the month and the winds are high. Above all the clatter and whoosh, the tenderest birdsong, longing and melodious. I don't recognise it. There it is – a starling.

Some of the hazel catkins are loose already – lemony-green ringlets. I tap one and a cloud of pollen surrounds my hand.

Cuckoo pint leaves

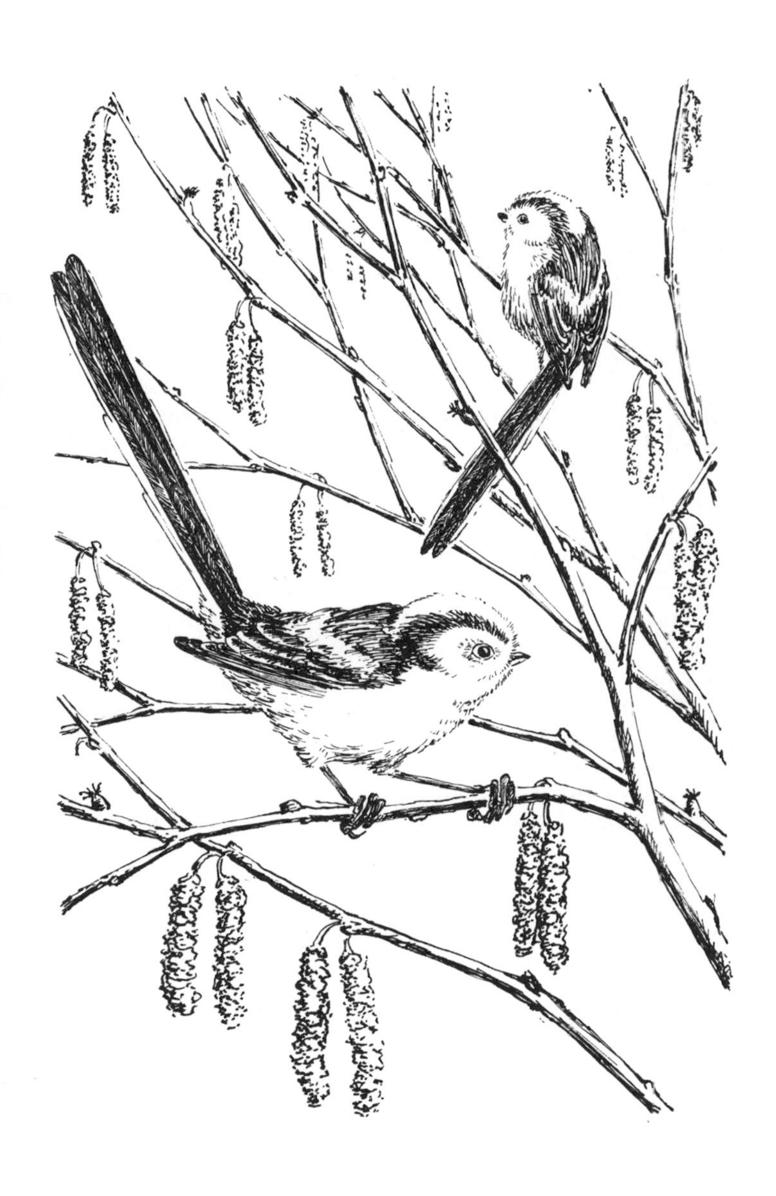

Long-tailed tits and hazel catkins

LONG-TAILED TITS

Long-tailed tits are the little Indian braves of the bird kingdom – our best chance of locating these distinctive pink, white and black tits is as they cross from one tree to another in single file.

The bird is agile, fast-moving and tiny – over half of its total length (14 cm) is its slender black and white tail. The actual body of the long-tailed tit is smaller than that of a wren.

It is rare to see just one long-tailed tit. They are usually in and out of the bushes (especially the birches and yews) in pairs or as part of a larger assembly either exclusively of long-tailed tits or of a mixed congregation.

Outside the breeding season and especially in mid-winter in the wooded fringes of the Downs, these mixed congregations consist typically of blue tits, great tits, goldfinches, greenfinches and goldcrests – sometimes even bullfinches. The congregations are always on the move and a line of long-tailed tits (often as many as 22) usually leads the procession from one tree to another, signalling all the way with a series of squeaks.

One of the bird world's most skilled nest builders, I suspect that the long-tailed tit is also one of the finest evaders of curious eyes. It was after three years of observation that I finally located an abandoned nest in thick bramble and ivy. The nest is a breathtakingly intricate oval dome of moss, cobwebs and hair and is thickly lined with feathers. The birds enter and leave through a small entrance hole to one side. Nesting begins in March and the white eggs (between 8 and 10) hatch in about 16 days. Careful watching of a likely spot with binoculars rewarded me with a glimpse of two young long-tailed tits – fluffy, short-tailed and nervous. I blinked and they had gone.

MARCH

3RD A few more celandine flowers are open this morning: these impatient ones are usually long-stemmed and insubstantial. Here's a clump of snowdrops - probably refugees from the gardens in Upper Belgrave Road.

It's warm and dewy and a charm of goldfinches flies from lime to lime, bouncing as though on invisible threads. When they land, they nod from side to side like clockwork toys. I count 14 goldfinches on one small lime. Below, an equally clockwork pied wagtail is hurrying along the pavement. He ventures into the road and scuttles back to the pavement when a car passes.

6TH It's sunny this afternoon but the wind is biting. I disturb two small tortoiseshell butterflies in the turf near the Water Tower. Nearby, a bumble-bee lands on a daisy and overwhelms it. Sweet violets are long-stemmed and quivering in the wind – a contrast with their earlier short-stemmed stiffness. Among the alexanders is a celandine with a 15 cm stem.

7TH A wren is singing loudly from the top of a small ash: usually wrens will choose a lower, more modest perch. Some of the ash buds are fatter and a few have split.

There's one hawthorn encircled by cuckoo pint with plain, rhubarb-like leaves and a neighbouring hawthorn surrounded by cuckoo pint with spotted leaves. What a variety of spots and blotches! Some are like carelessly thrown black ink and others are dotted with a delicate precision.

11TH Blue tits are excited this morning, fast-flying in pairs and circling the hawthorns. They enter the bushes with a flying curve and a rising flourish of song.

Along Westbury Road, dark-leaved celandine flowers are half open and cupped like water lilies.

17TH There are two green anemone buds above their shaggy leaves under a hawthorn and the cliff path is lined with a white tapestry of barren strawberry flowers.

Amber and yellow wallflowers are in bloom along the Gorge side and in the wood above them the male catkins of the goat willow are alight with yellow pollen.

On the Avon Gorge rocks, one wayfaring tree is in flower already. Elsewhere, in the wooded fringes of the Downs, wayfaring leaves are just parting to reveal the tightly-packed flowerheads. These new leaves have a pearly bloom in the sunshine.

Green-fingered leaves are prising open more horse chestnut buds. Underneath them, last year's ungathered conkers have split and pink shoots of new trees are coiling into the ground.

The tight elm rosebuds have loosened into carmine flowers and from a distance, the elms themselves have a rose-pink aura.

20**TH** The sun has enticed two brimstone butterflies to a purposeful flight. Brimstone – what a harsh name for these flying primroses. Appropriately, the banks near the butterflies' flightpaths are dotted with actual primroses and this flamboyant clump opposite the Zoo has 35 blooms and six buds.

Nearby there is a patch of scentless dog violets under the brambles: their popular name, 'blue mice', is more endearing.

Bumble-bee

23**RD** The day of the dunnock! From three bushes in the Dumps, three dunnocks are singing their gossipy songs. Other birds are temporarily silent.

There are blue puddles of Buxbaum's speedwell near the Observatory and green and yellow lakes of celandines in Fairyland.

The large-leaved green alkanet has an incongruously small flower. More blue nearby – a solitary wild forget-me-not among the daisies.

Some of the elm roses have become rosettes of green seeds, and neatly-ridged elm leaves are fanning out from the end of the branches.

There is a dead fox under a hawthorn in the Granny Downs.

25TH Billows of blackthorn blossom along the Promenade and, under the beech ride, thousands of baby beech trees like large clover leaves.

One young lime on Clifton Green is full of leaf.

Above the bushes of the Dumps, the kestrel hovers and then shoots out of the wind like a flying crossbow.

Little stars of chickweed are wide open around the limes and ash trees of Westbury Road, and the buds of the chestnut leaves gleam like forests of light amongst the dark branches.

30TH These diminutive daffodil flowers in the ash wood could almost pass for wild although one has disgraced itself by being double. Five wood-pigeons are balancing on the topmost twigs of an ash and two of them are pecking at the emerging ash flowers. One bird loses balance and there is a great deal of flapping and rearrangement.

Two of the smaller silver birches are in leaf, larger trees remain bare.

There is an outbreak of 32 honey-brown earthballs beside Westbury Road.

31ST **7.30 a.m.** A dusting of snow this morning. I look over the Gorge side to the warm yellow of the wallflowers and I can smell them.

A robin has part of his territory here and his boundary inspection includes a conscientious scurry up a rock incline.

The kestrel is perched on a nearby hawthorn, watching me and puffed up against the cold.

FOXES

Late workers and early risers throughout the city are probably used to encounters with Bristol's streetwise foxes. It takes a second or two to realise that it's not a dog or cat and usually, while we're making this adjustment, the fox is watching us with those acute amber eyes and a dismissive wave of the tail.

Those of us who live or work near the Downs may meet them just before dawn as the foxes return to their earths in the large gardens of Clifton, Sneyd Park and Redland. Not that the foxes give the impression of hurry to be home. Between the hours of six and seven, they seem to idle about, curling round the bottom of pillar-boxes, lurking in gateways, stretching out on garage roofs and sometimes leaning against the warm doors of the local launderette.

Urban foxes normally rest during the day and forage by night and perhaps the best time to encounter a fox on the Downs would be between one and four o'clock in the morning, especially on a warm, wet night when earthworms and slugs are easy to come by. On the other hand, plenty of foxes have been seen at about six in the morning – on the Granny Downs, sitting in the middle of the Seven Sisters, trotting along the Circular Road, or on the rocks at Black Rock Gully.

Foxes visit all parts of the Downs, including the Promenade and the Observatory, and Suspension Bridge attendants are used to seeing them sauntering across the bridge itself in the early hours of the morning.

Most of us have mixed feelings about foxes. Those barks and screams of the mid-winter mating season can drive would-be sleepers to distraction and there's always a neighbour or friend who has lost a beloved pet to the cunning of the fox. Their habit of foraging in dustbins is equally maddening and their musty smell isn't endearing if it affects our home or garden.

In the open air of the Downs, however the smell of foxes is less offensive – even slightly exciting. It's hard not to feel a fleeting admiration for that auburn coat, that nerve and ability to survive and that 'Frankly, I don't give a damn' arrogance.

Fox and primroses

APRIL

2ND An elderly gentleman is sitting on a blue and white garden chair next to a telescope trained on the Avon Gorge rocks. He lets me look through his telescope and I have a breathtaking view of the female peregrine falcon. Two jackdaws are sitting on a hawthorn by the telescope, their backs to the Gorge, staring at an ice-cream van.

3RD The grass is bright green and the sky is divided in colour between pure blue and dark, brooding grey.

More silver birches are in leaf: a dainty leaf for such a sturdy tree.

Many of the new horse chestnut leaves and buds have been torn away and scattered by last night's gales.

I hear the mocking laugh of the green woodpecker and the rain begins again. I'm sure there's a faint rainbow.

4TH Clumps of white sweet violets flower alongside the blue and several of the flowers are a mixture of both colours. A bee-fly is visiting one of the flowers like a miniature brown hummingbird.

6TH Germander speedwell is nestling close to the ferny leaves of cow parsley under the hawthorns. As I pass, I disturb two bullfinches bathing in a puddle.

Wood-pigeons rove over the turf near the Seven Sisters, feasting on the new shoots of clover.

8TH 7.00 a.m. Black Rock Gully. Two long-tailed tits fly past me, both with feathers in their beaks and thus unable to make their usual flight-calls. I can hear the high whirring sound of their wings.

10TH The first cowslips in flower by the Seven Sisters. **9.00 a.m.** A light snowfall.

15TH More cowslips, on the grassy bank behind the Water Tower. Grapefruit-yellow dandelions are in flower over the entire Downs.

17TH So many cowslips now. I can see them easily in the early morning light: theirs is a pale greeny-yellow, softer than that of dandelions and buttercups. Nearby, spring cinquefoil (rare and a harsh yellow) is dotted in the grass.

APRIL

20TH There are eight bluebells in flower in Fairyland. One is slender with just one bell.

The whitebeams on the Gorge side are an astonishing acid-green and many of the hawthorns seem to have come into leaf overnight. Some oak buds have split and the catkins of the male flowers are cascading out.

There are thousands of shades of green on the Downs today.

21ST A kestrel is sitting on top of a lime watching firemen on an extending ladder free a large blue stunter kite from a tree. The wind blows the kite towards Redland and seconds later the kestrel soars off in the opposite direction.

22ND Buxbaum's speedwell is circling the lime trees like a blue shadow. It's that time when the daisies are red-rimmed and when celandines, buttercups, speedwell and violets flower together.

The shade of this hawthorn is home to the mauvy-pink cuckoo flower. Moving closer I can see a wood anemone among the rusty beech leaves. It looked from a distance like a bit of white tissue-paper, thrown away.

Wood anemone

A male chaffinch is pecking at the ground under this hawthorn. Suddenly he launches into the air, moves as though to land in the bush, stops, hovers and returns to the ground. I have noticed the indecisive behaviour of chaffinches before.

There are four white doves on the grass near the White Tree roundabout.

23RD I stop to look at a large black ladybird with two red spots on a leaf of garlic mustard and a male orange tip butterfly settles nearby.

Under a silver birch, a circle of hooded cuckoo pint spathes: a woodland gathering of the Ku Klux Klan.

Good gracious, the well-preserved remains of 14 stinkhorn fungi in a hazel copse. I've never encountered such an abundance in so small a space: the smell when they were fresh must have been revolting.

Under a holly tree the heart-shaped beginnings of black bryony are reaching out to clasp the lower branches and begin their long upward journey.

24TH The ferocity of nesting birds! I wonder at the agitation of a male blackbird and see that he is attempting to scare a weasel away from a bush. I presume the female blackbird is on the nest there.

Later, I see a long-tailed tit defy and scold a magpie.

25TH Here are five open spathes of cuckoo pint. There are three purple spadices, one yellow and one olive-green.

Nearby is a handsome, creamy St. George's mushroom – two days late.

27TH All the daisy buds are closed in the rain – pink dots in the grass.

A starling is yaffling like a green woodpecker.

28TH Jackdaws are riding the wind above the Gorge. They fly up as though tossed at random by a giant hand and then land on the rocks elegantly and with precision.

29TH The last blackthorn buds are loosening into flower in Black Rock Gully. Above them, wood-pigeons are engaging in that soaring and flapping performance which looks ecstatic and sounds like wet canvas in a high wind.

There are fragments of a pale-blue bird's egg under this hawthorn.

The transparent leaves of the copper beech are all but weightless when I cup them in my hand: it's like cradling a shadow.

THE PEREGRINE FALCONS

The stunning fact is that in the middle of our city – in the Avon Gorge – and in sight of visitors to the Bristol Downs, we have a nesting pair of peregrine falcons. The peregrine is considered to be one of the world's most spectacular birds and it is certainly our most magnificent bird of prey, now specially protected by law.

To watch these birds above the Gorge, hovering, circling, plummeting out of the sky – or even to see them sitting on the rocks, methodically preening and cleaning their toes, is to join the frustrating attempts to describe their beauty, power and mastery of flight.

These hunting birds kill in the air, flying like a bullet to do so and reaching speeds of up to 180 miles per hour. Peregrines kill by breaking the neck or back of their victims with a blow from their talons. In the Avon Gorge their usual prey are pigeons and starlings. The corpse is taken to a 'plucking-tree' where the flesh is torn to fragments.

Peregrines are capable of killing much more formidable birds; in November 1936 the Bristol Museum received the body of a raven killed by a peregrine falcon in the Avon Gorge.

A recent encounter with a peregrine haunts me. I was standing in the woods near the cliffs, watching three baby blackcaps sitting in triangle formation on the branches of a dog rose. The birds were squeaking and quivering for food and a parent bird was prospecting in a nearby ash.

Suddenly a peregrine swept up from the Gorge below – the embodiment of speed and power and a staggering contrast with the insubstantial, nervy birds I was observing. All four blackcaps ducked their heads and froze and so, for a second, did I.

All watchers of the falcon have a symbolic image of the bird: the folded-winged stoop to a kill; the acrobatic passing of food from one bird to another in mid-air; a peregrine swooping out of the early morning mist surrounding the Suspension Bridge; the male returning at dusk from Avonmouth clutching a snow-white dove. Watch the peregrines cross the Gorge, dropping low from the Downs' cliffs and rising to their 'plucking-tree' across the river – effortlessly floating upwards, in collusion with the air.

Peregrine falcon

MAY

1ST Here are the buttercups. The cow parsley is beginning to spread white lace around the hawthorn bushes. A sound like crickets – it's young blue tits begging for food and vibrating their triangular wings.

A wide, empty blue sky above. No swifts yet.

The hawthorn is in bud.

2ND A few ramsons are flowering, romantic white stars in the ride behind the ash wood. Every bridal bouquet would contain these flowers but for the inconvenient smell of garlic.

Nesting birds are behaving with purpose and direction and even the wood-pigeons are flying with style, hovering like doves and plunging like hawks.

5TH The swifts are back. An advance guard of two over the Avon Gorge: tomorrow they will be soaring all over the Downs.

There are cowslips throughout this meadow grass and this one, under the ash, has a stem of 31 cm.

Here is a green-winged orchid, 10 cm high, purple and with green wing-like veins on its helmet arrangement of petals.

This is a good day for firsts: the first hawthorn blossom – white. Pink usually comes later. The first tissue-like rock-roses.

7TH Hundreds of wild strawberry flowers on this grassy bank behind the Water Tower.

8TH **6.10 a.m.** I can hear the cuckoo. In my 20 or so years in Bristol, I've never heard it in the woods on this side of the Avon Gorge.

9TH New beech leaves are soft and downy to touch, like the top of a baby's head.

A valley of dog violets in the shade near the Circular Road: thousands of flowers. As I kneel to look closely, I can hear a baby robin hissing for food in the brambles nearby.

White layers of sweet-scented spring. The cow parsley is shoulder-high, reaching to the white hawthorn blossom. Above this, the creamy horse chestnut spires.

There is cuckoo spit* on the lower leaves of this herb robert.

10TH A female common blue butterfly, head down at the end of a long blade of grass. I put my finger close to it and the butterfly crawls onto it, opens its wings and flies away.

A patch of four-leaved clovers – so many it devalues the currency.

A kestrel shoots out of a horse chestnut on the Granny Downs followed by two angry starlings – and here's a mistle thrush attacking a crow. The thrush is diving at the crow from a high branch of the ash and is scolding and clacking like machine-gun fire.

11TH The breeze is carrying the fragrance of the wallflowers to the Sea Walls. There is a cormorant flying towards Shirehampton and a heron standing on the mud-flats on the Leigh Woods side of the Gorge.

Swallows are flying low around the ash wood.

12TH Here's a horse chestnut near Wills Hall with white spires as long as lupins.

At last the plane trees are coming into leaf and the female flowers are hanging like pom-poms at the tips of the shoots.

14TH The cerise flowers of common vetch are dotted throughout this grassland: just one flower is open on each plant and the leaflets curl above the flower like the wings of a dark angel. Yellow rattle looks like a poor man's cowslip.

3.30 p.m. The peregrine falcons are hunting in the Gorge, flying from nest to 'plucking-tree' with breathtaking ease.

16TH The willow warbler is back on the ash by Black Rock Gully and there's another in the oak near the Zoo. What a wistful song.

Wayfaring trees are decked with creamy blossom.

A miniature buttercup near the Seven Sisters is only 5 mm across and is a pale yellow, much closer to the shade of our

---

* This is the froth produced by the common frog hopper to protect its young from drying out and from predators.

butter today. Butter must have been alarmingly bright when the flower was originally named.

The air is electric with swifts this morning.

Willow warbler

18TH Germander speedwell is an intense turquoise-blue. The bottom flower on the stalk is the first to open and the first to die, fading to an attractive shade of violet.

A jay is flying between chestnuts on the Granny Downs.

Cathedrals of horse chestnut spires and the white is now joined by the later flowering red.

It's the time of dandelion clocks, buttercups and fragrant, snowy hawthorn.

The elm seeds have turned to orange and the trees look dusty. By contrast, the copper beeches are glossy and this one, near the White Tree, is burgundy-pink.

There's a tiny new copper beech under this parent tree, its first adult leaves a perfect colour match.

There are daisies everywhere today.

20TH 6.45 a.m. On top of a hawthorn in the ash wood, a greenfinch is repeating a bell-like sequence. The bird's tail quivers with the song.

What a peculiar performance behind this bush. A male blackbird is hopping in front of a female with his back feathers ruffed up as though injured. The female looks interested but not especially concerned. Probably a courtship ritual.

Salad burnet is an intricate plant. It is apparently becoming rare as it's popular in packets of wildflower seeds. There's plenty of it here, though, near the Zoo.

A blackcap and a chiffchaff are on the same whitebeam overlooking Black Rock Gully. Each bird sings in turn – the loud melody of the blackcap and then the monotonous repetition of the chiffchaff. I have met this complementary partnership of birds before on the Downs and farther afield.

A coal tit is busy in the nearby brambles.

Two mallards fly towards Clifton, using the old elm ride as a runway.

25TH The foliage of an elder has been replaced by a cobweb-like grey gauze. Not one leaf remains. Inside the gauze I can see thousands of small ermine moth larvae in their tents, writhing and climbing.

26TH The horse chestnut leaves are darker and coarser and the red blossom is falling onto the paths.

29TH 10.00 p.m. The hawthorn blossom is black and white in the moonlight and its fragrance is cooler.

Two bats are using this corner of the Downs as a skating-rink: mad black butterflies, drawn by the moon.

30TH The Downs are golden with buttercups this morning.

THE HAWTHORNS

Hawthorn – 'May' blossom on the Downs – is Bristol's finest flower show. Densely borne, sweet-smelling blossoms of white, pink and red. Sometimes, where several hawthorns grow together, there seem to be three or four shades on one bush.

And for those who know the Downs all year round, these hawthorns offer more than this fragrant carnival.

Throughout the winter, the bare shapes of these bushes are tough wooden sculptures of wrestling limbs, clasped hands and outstretched palms: from a distance, a bonsai embodiment of strength and grace. Hawthorn berries remain until the spring and redwings and fieldfares are among the birds to benefit from them during the colder months.

As March progresses, so do the hawthorn leaves, spreading over dark branches like dustings of green snow – the older the tree, the slower to leaf. Soon whole bushes seem to burst into leaf overnight and one of the sudden delights of April is the sight of these apple-green bushes against a grey sky.

Blossom can last until June and often ends dramatically as gales strip the petals, exposing tiny green berries.

These berries – haws – are red by late summer and are as thick as the spring blossom.

In the wilder areas of the Downs, too, many of the bushes are apparently home to autumn berries borne by other bushes and climbing plants which grow in and through the hawthorn umbrellas. Elderberries, blackberries, holly berries, ivy berries, spindle fruits and rose-hips add a complexity of colour and detail to their hawthorn 'hosts'. Black bryony with its glistening scarlet berries frequently twines through hawthorns and white bryony also threads its tendrils through the bushes. The red, orange, yellow and green berries of white bryony are like strings of children's beads hanging from the branches.

Mistletoe has its hold on one old hawthorn bush and eight clusters hang throughout the year, the berries often lasting until May.

Also in the wilder areas of the Downs, the autumn hawthorns are covered with the fluffy white seedheads of wild clematis, popularly known as 'old man's beard': this gives the appearance of a strange and highly selective fall of snow.

Hawthorn and swifts

All year round, hawthorns offer protection to the birds of the Downs – especially to tits, finches, blackbirds and robins. Wild flowers, too, are not forgotten. Look under hawthorn bushes in the spring for patches of sweet violets, cuckoo pint, anemones, celandines, cuckoo flower, herb bennet and for the lace-like cow parsley which sometimes stretches as far as the lower branches of the bush itself.

JUNE

1ST The yellow month: buttercups, bird's-foot-trefoil, rock-roses, dandelions, yellow rattle and three lingering cowslips. The hawthorn is at its best and the white and pink blossom is like blotted lipstick.

Thousands of tiny apple-green conker cases have replaced the horse chestnut blossom.

2ND There is a clump of deep-yellow horseshoe vetch on this rock face and, nestling in the crevices, the fragrant basil thyme – considered by some to be one of our most attractive wild flowers, able to cure rheumatism and cheer the depressed.

4TH Gales and dark skies. Many of the embryonic conkers are strewn on the grass.

6TH What's this unusual colour on a bramble leaf? It's a moth with the primrose-yellow of the brimstone butterfly. Later I discover that this is the brimstone moth.

An orange-chested baby robin is watching me, sitting in the diamond criss-cross of the wire above the cliff at Black Rock Gully.

There seems to be a bee in every buttercup this morning.

7TH The long grass is a rippling bronze ocean: ox-eye daisies float on the surface and sorrel is poking through it like the masts of a spangled shipwreck. Swifts fly low over the wavy grass, sometimes curving in fluid arcs, sometimes flapping and darting like bats.

8TH Drizzle and cold. Parent starlings are harassed by their young. In Fairyland, three blackcaps are sitting in a triangle on a dog rose bush, cheeping and quivering for food. Nearby I can hear baby robins hissing under the brambles.

9TH 6.15 a.m. Early morning in Black Rock Gully. Dark and damp and there's smoke-like mist rising from the Avon Gorge Woods.

Why do pigeons engage in that soaring and flapping business more often when it's damp?

The kestrel is flying low – I can see the chunkiness of his body. The swifts are low-flying, too, and I can hear the swish of their wings.

JUNE

10TH 6.30 a.m. A skylark* is hovering above the meadow grass, pouring out those fast, bubbly notes.

11TH In the turf of Observatory Hill, the lavender-blue clary – such a colour!

12TH Only one gull in the sky this morning and it's being chased by a swift. When the swift gets too close, the gull rounds on it – but the swift returns and follows the gull's circles and sweeps.

From my reading, I note that Richard Jefferies wonders if violets are sown by ants, which apparently carry violet seeds into their nests. In the woods above Black Rock Gully, there are two dog violets in flower, growing from the top of an ants' nest.

13TH There is a board by the side of the Gorge with the latest news of the peregrine falcon family. Today's announcement is, 'Young birds starting to fly'. One bird is flying but it seems that the other is holding back. The main danger is crash-landing on the rocks.

15TH The Dumps are a meadow. Creamy hedge bedstraw is drifting over the rocks and dog roses are an exquisite pink.

Dog rose

---

* There are nesting skylarks at Ashton Court.

JUNE

Elder flowers are like huge pearl brooches.

Here's one flowering foxglove and dozens of dropwort blossoms – tiaras of coral and pearl.

Common blue butterflies are dancing in the sun and I can hear the hot rasping of grasshoppers.

A scuffle in the grass and a tiny frog moves away from my hand to the safety of a crevice in the rocks.

Here are five shaggy parasol mushrooms under a hawthorn: a spider has woven a lace tablecloth over one of them.

18TH Four common spotted orchids – crinolines of pink and white. And here, three bumble-bees on a stalk! It's a bee orchid – its flowers perfect miniature bees.

24TH The cherries on the Granny Downs are ripe enough to eat.

Midsummer and such rain. What's this? Probably a wren flying in front of me to perch on a shrub near the White Tree. No – it's a treecreeper.

26TH Here is yellow kidney vetch on the rocks of Black Rock Gully. Some of the flower-heads have died and the sepals around the pods have swollen like plump white pincushions.

A young robin is preening itself in the sun, sitting on the top of this wooden seat. It's an unusually ragged and puffed-up performance.

There's a nasty black accumulation of peacock caterpillars on the nettles near the Water Tower.

28TH **6.00 a.m.** There's a squirrel sitting on a boundary stone by Ladies Mile, eating a large oak apple.

29TH Yet more yellow at the end of the month: silverweed and the greeny-yellow buds of lady's bedstraw. Vivid lemon biting stonecrop is part of a yellow, purple and orange patchwork with the lichen and thyme on the rocks in the Dumps – and the stars of perforate St. John's-wort are a distinctive ochre. Some of the berries of cuckoo pint are orange already.

30TH Fairy flax is twinkling in the meadow grass and quaking grass is an intricacy of burnished copper.

The lime buds will soon be open; their cream bracts are hanging under the dark leaves like ballet shoes.

BIRD'S-FOOT-TREFOIL, YELLOW RATTLE, ROCK-ROSES AND A COWSLIP

Three yellow flowers to represent June and high summer: bird's-foot-trefoil, yellow rattle and rock-rose. One cowslip has a place here, too, because the cowslips on the Downs often linger on into early June.

Cowslips have everything in their favour: they are a lovely flower to see, to touch, to smell and, in days of former abundance, to taste in salads and wine. The cowslips on the Downs vary in height from the 4 cm stems of the miniatures near the Seven Sisters to 30 cm or more. In full flower, the plant is like a bunch of hanging keys and many of the folk names reflect this: 'Our Lady's keys', 'Key of Heaven', 'St. Peter's keys'. Before dying the flower turns its head to the sun like an outstretched hand, asking for more.

The Downs house a substantial patch of yellow rattle on the fringes of the woodland near the Circular Road. Yellow rattle has an absurd, rabbit-like appearance although, to be charitable, the new flowers could pass for a poor man's cowslip. The whole plant, spear-like leaves, petals and sepals, has a hard, papery feel. Later, the seeds inside the capsule do actually rattle as the wind blows the grass (or when we shake them). Sometimes this rattle may be caused by ladybirds and ants sheltering in the pods.

Bird's-foot-trefoil is largely responsible for the golding of the football pitches and meadow areas of the Downs once the early summer buttercup extravaganza has passed. The flower changes colour three times – from the scarlet buds, to the glossy yellow flowers (neatly etched with red), and the burnt-orange of the fading blossoms.

Over 70 folk names attempt to describe bird's-foot-trefoil – from the insulting 'crow-toes' to the arguably over-exalted 'God Almighty's thumb and finger'. The naturalist Richard Jefferies referred to the flower most appropriately, perhaps, as the 'bird's-foot lotus'.*

Often growing alongside bird's-foot-trefoil in the Dumps and rocky areas of the Downs, rock-roses are scentless and are better not touched as the tissue-like yellow petals are frail

---

* "Wild Flowers" in *Under the Acorns* by Richard Jefferies, (Horizon Books 1982).

and quick to detach. The rock-rose is a flower of colour, pattern and symmetry and its appeal is to the sight and to the imagination. The buds have an oriental, lantern-like beauty and the whole flower closes at night and in wet weather. Look at the flower in full sunlight, however, and the core of orange stamens and illuminated petals will leave you in no doubt of the appeal of this flower: the rock-rose is in partnership with the sun.

JULY

1ST The leaves of the copper beeches are the colour of molasses. Ash-keys hang down in green clusters and the winged seeds of the sycamores are flushed with strawberry-pink.

From a distance the Downs are a uniform green. Close-up, however, the turf is an embroidery of pink and white clover, daisies and bird's-foot-trefoil.

A red admiral is sunning itself on a stone near the Water Tower and nearby, on a bramble in shade, there is a scarlet tiger moth. It is mercilessly hot and the birds are silent.

2ND 6.00 a.m. A magpie morning! There is a young magpie (short tail, long legs, screeching complaints) under an ash in Ladies Mile. Elsewhere, other protesting young magpies are being supervised by their parents and in the long grass near the Zoo there is a noisy group of ten.

I stand holding the railings at the edge of the Gorge, waiting for the peregrine falcons to appear. There is a scuffling in the brambles below my hand and a young robin surfaces by my thumb. This is too close even for a robin and the bird dips back into the brambles and reappears further along the railings. One tall Aaron's rod overlooks the Gorge, its alert yellow flowers surveying the cliffs.

Chiffchaffs are having trouble starting this morning. One chiffchaff in the walnut tree manages 12 repetitions and then falls silent for several minutes before attempting another eight. Here is a wild carrot flower – a lace-like arrangement of white blossoms with one red flower in the middle like a drop of blood on a napkin.

3RD 7.00 a.m. There is a peregrine falcon on a hawthorn near the Dumps; it is the adult male and he is watching me as carefully as I am watching him. I move closer and he flies off, landing in an ash on Ladies Mile.

Twenty minutes later I am standing on the edge of the cliffs and see the falcon approach, flying low over the meadow grass and carrying the limp body of a young starling.

4TH The wind is carrying the honey smell of linden blossom and at the entrance to Hollybush Lane there are two limes with thousands of loose, fragrant blonde ringlets.

JULY

5TH **6.15 a.m.** A green woodpecker is pecking the turf by the White Tree roundabout and two baby squirrels are crossing Westbury Road, just missing the zebra crossing.

Eight goldfinches cross the meadow grass, twittering pleasantly as they fly. Below them, two linnets search the ground, the breast of the male opal-pink in the early morning sun.

The chiffchaff has more stamina this morning.

7.30 p.m. Swifts are swarming like flying ants over the Granny Downs.

6TH **6.45 a.m.** There are two peregrine falcons on hawthorns near the Dumps this morning. I watch them soar upwards and circle over the old elm ride, suddenly dropping to hover over the meadow grass.

The pointed heads of hundreds of crow garlic flowers are thrusting through the grass like the spears of an underground army.

10TH **6.00 a.m.** A wren is singing in Fairyland: dry leaves fall in clusters around it, disturbed by the vibrations of the song.

There is a fox in front of me on the cliff path, an unusually scraggy creature. Later our paths meet again and the fox limps away, stiff and lame.

12TH Under a hawthorn on the Granny Downs – agrimony – tiny spires of yellow stars, one after the other up the stem like a rocket trail.

There is a magnificent colony of meadow crane's-bill near Worrall Road. Large blue flowers – a feast for the eyes.

Ranks of fragrant musk thistle in the Dumps, ferny dill and lemon layers of lady's bedstraw.

The swollen pods of yellow rattle rustle when the wind blows, and crunch underfoot. I shake a pod and a ladybird climbs out.

Two yellow-faced baby blue tits huddle and shiver on the lower branches of a lime. Underneath, a marbled white butterfly sways on the tip of a long stem of dry grass.

There are four poppies in the corn-coloured meadow by the Circular Road.

Near the Observatory, gorse pods burst in the sun, crackling as though on fire.

Meadow crane's-bill

13TH **6.10 a.m.** There is a rainbow over the old elm ride and a peregrine falcon on top of an ash. Suddenly a rook hurtles out of the same ash and the falcon leaps into the air behind it. A loud and dizzying battle begins, framed by the rainbow. The falcon chases the rook twice around the ash, then on to the Water Tower, to the Seven Sisters and away over the Granny Downs.

I peer into the dark canopy of a yew and a fox peers back at me.

14TH **6.00 a.m.** There are 143 starlings, four goldfinches, two magpies and a black-headed gull roving over the recently mown turf around the Seven Sisters.

A young blackbird is standing on the pavement near the Water Tower. The female parent bird appears, a portion of worm in her beak. The young bird runs to her and starts to sing a tentative, plaintive melody. The parent listens, her head on one side. Suddenly the song is over, the parent stuffs the worm into the young bird's mouth and both of them hasten back to the bushes.

11.30 a.m. The kestrel is hovering over the meadow grass and there are six peacock butterflies on the buddleia.

This heat may be making the small birds ratty. A pigeon has just soared out of an ash tree and a sparrow shot out of a bush below and pulled its tail feathers.

15TH There is a pyramidal orchid on a bank: rosy-mauve and two-toned. Nearby, a pool of harebells.

17TH **5.45 a.m.** No lovelier smell than linden blossom after the rain. Pale young mistle thrushes have positioned themselves at intervals over the mown turf.

There is a heron standing in the middle of the football pitch nearest to the Sea Walls.

Chaffinches are singing loudly this morning.

I find three double buttercups near the Seven Sisters.

20TH The colour purple: mallow, bramble blossom, everlasting pea, musk thistles, thyme, rosebay willow-herb, knapweed, clover and betony.

As I walk through the long grass, I disturb meadow brown butterflies. They flutter a short distance and then tumble back below the surface of the grass.

Common blue butterflies are clustering around the sweet-smelling marjoram on the rocks of Black Rock Gully.

A six-spot burnet moth lands on a knapweed. Further down the rocks, centaury is a modest almond-pink and yellow-wort is a defiant yellow.

25TH The birds are silent except for an occasional outburst of wren or dunnock and the restless calling of the goldcrests in the top branches of the pines.

29TH Hundreds of earthballs in the turf this morning and here is a collection of fairies' bonnets – enchanting fungi.

31ST The conker cases are promisingly plump.

Some of the lime seeds have swollen into hard green balls. Before they ripen to festive pink and orange, spindle berries are the colour of cooking apples.

Where are the swifts?

BUTTERFLIES

Not just creatures of high summer, butterflies patrol the Downs for as many as ten months of the year – starting with the brimstone which makes brief, tropical appearances on warm February afternoons – and often ending with the lonely gliding flight of the peacock across the snowy clematis seedheads of November.

For those who like lists, these are the butterflies most often encountered on the Downs, the meadow areas and Dumps are especially rewarding: speckled wood, marbled white, red admiral, small tortoiseshell, peacock, brimstone, common blue, painted lady, orange tip, meadow brown, comma, large white, small white.

The marbled white is perhaps the king (and queen) of the Downs' butterflies. Large (wingspan 58 mm), and elegant, this butterfly is a regal flyer, slow-flapping and unhurried. The clear black and white markings, especially of the male butterfly, make it a breathtaking complement to any flower and perfect with the purple knapweed or deep-blue scabious. Earlier naturalists who often brought poetic and mystical considerations to bear on their observations were fascinated by fortuitous natural colour combinations like these.

It's unusual to see the marbled white crossing wide expanses of turf on the Downs in the way that the peacocks, tortoiseshells and whites do; the marbled white stays close to its chosen area – often even returning to the same blade of long grass to rest.

The blue of the male common blue (the female is brown) defies description – is it violet or sky-blue? Apart from the fact that the shade actually varies between butterflies, the problem is that usually all we see of this fast-moving little butterfly is a flickering impression of blue.

Common blues love the sun. If the sky is a mixture of sun and cloud, stand at the edge of the meadow area and watch these butterflies leave their plants and dance up into the sun the very second the cloud passes over and the sunlight reappears. Often, three or four common blues meet and fly together, climbing the air, one over the other.

A day-flying moth rather than a butterfly, the six-spot burnet is another lover of sunshine and the moth's black and red colouring is a stunning if not conventionally fortuitous colour combination with the summer flowers. The bright colours are a warning to predators – all of the life stages of this moth contain cyanide.

A note about orchids

The orchid in the illustration is the pyramidal which flowered in 1991 after an apparent absence of 70 years. The Downs are also home to other orchids – the bee orchid, autumn lady's tresses, the common spotted orchid and, in 1992 for the first time ever recorded, the nationally scarce green-winged orchid.

Marbled white and common blue butterflies, six-spot burnet moth, bird's-foot-trefoil and a pyramidal orchid

AUGUST

1ST 7.00 a.m. The football pitches have not been mown for a while and the dandelion seedheads are full and fluffy. Clinging to the centre of many of them is a bee – sometimes two. I count 80 bee-occupied heads on this pitch and I can see many more.

A blackbird is making insistent alarm calls – probably to warn that the kestrel is about. What is strange is that he is sitting less than a metre away from the kestrel on the same branch of the dead hawthorn.

5TH 6.30 a.m. There are dozens of goldfinches feeding with the starlings on the buttercups and dandelion heads.

A wood-pigeon flies above me, his wings creaking as though in need of oil.

10TH The grass has been cut and the cobwebs in it are shimmering with dew. Here's a male and a female common blue on the same scabious.

A robin scurries back into the hawthorn as I pass, still in hiding for his summer moult. Only the magpies are noisy today.

15TH It's hot and butterflies are flying amongst the knapweed, thistle, crow garlic and the straw-like grass. I can see marbled white butterflies, common blues, meadow browns, cinnebar moths and six-spot burnet moths.

Three marbled white butterflies are trying to land on one small head of purple knapweed – playing I'm the king of the castle! And a bonus – here, opposite the Zoo is the flightpath of an enormous dragonfly.

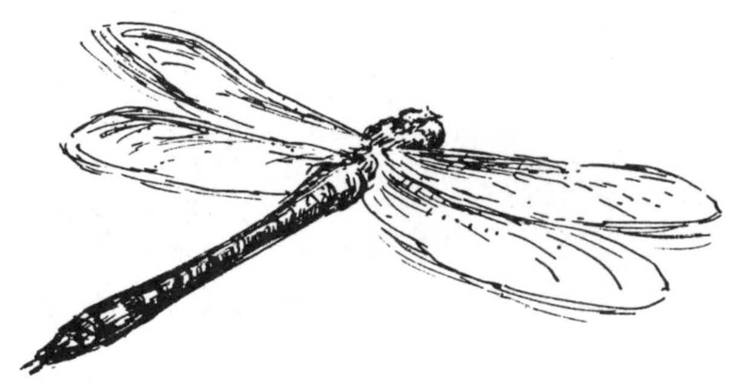

Dragonfly

AUGUST

19TH The garlics have lost the strong smell they had in the spring but they are still attracting bees and common blue butterflies. The rare field garlic is here, on Durdham Down, and its flowers are like mint humbugs.

20TH The fluffy seeds of rosebay willowherb are shining in the sun.

Most of the lime seeds have hardened to little greeny-brown nuts and papery yellow bracts are surrounding the trees like a rehearsal for autumn.

Squirrels are shaking the hazels, searching them for nuts.

Young jackdaws follow their parents, flapping their wings and begging to be fed.

Wild clematis flowers are a fragrant cream blanket over the hawthorns in the wilder parts of the Downs.

22ND 6.30 a.m. Gulls are on one side of the football pitch, rooks on the other. Each set of birds faces the other like black and white chessmen.

Black Rock Gully. A baby green woodpecker is on the rocks a few metres away from me. He's not at all smart and is a far cry from the exotic and arrogant parent birds. A robin joins us, sitting on the wire. We wait. Suddenly the woodpecker is off over the valley with an unevenly dipping flight and a not very finely-tuned yaffle.

25TH 7.00 a.m. In a circle around a hawthorn copse small yellow snails are moving from the turf to the long grass below the bushes. Hundreds of snails, horns all pointing towards the copse. I check. This isn't happening anywhere else.

2.30 p.m. I go back to look at the snails. The copse is full of them. During the morning the surrounding grass was mown.

26TH It's surprising to see a brimstone butterfly this morning. I associate the brimstone with the early spring and it seems out of place among the ripening berries. I've heard that the brimstone was once called 'the butter-coloured fly' and this actually gives us our lovely word butterfly.

27TH The first ripe blackberries.

Looking over the Gorge to Leigh Woods, I notice that the Gorge side trees are already touched with gold.

On a rock near the Gorge is a slender slug, about 10 cm long: the top third is striped like a tiger.
Knopper gall* on this oak looks like wrinkled green socks.

28TH Cold and wet. High winds. The beech leaves rustle with an autumn paperiness.

30TH Soft new leaves are still unfolding at the end of the branches of the plane trees.
Bees circle the lime trees.
Some of the yew berries are a deep, translucent red.

---

* knopper gall – this deformity affects the acorns of the English Oak and is caused by the gall wasp *andricus quercuscalicis*, an insect which has only become common in Britain during the last 20 years, having travelled over from France.

THE GREEN WOODPECKER

The green woodpecker is a formidable bird – the largest of British woodpeckers and the most flamboyant. The crimson crown, green wings and yellow rump give the bird a tropical appearance and recently, while I was watching one a little boy asked me if he could help me catch the parrot.

There's a good chance of seeing this bird on the turf of the Downs, especially in the winter. It's much more difficult to spot the green woodpecker in a tree unless a casual drumming betrays the location.

Throughout January and February, I observed a green woodpecker in the same spot near Ladies Mile – hour after hour. She (females have a black 'moustache', males a red one) was pecking at worm-casts to get at the ants in the soil and I used binoculars to see her scoop up the ants with her long sticky tongue.

It's fascinating to observe how much human proximity the green woodpecker will tolerate. At 15 metres the bird is visibly aware of the presence of humans (or dogs) and stops feeding, beak jutting into the air, assessing the situation. If people venture closer, the bird often pecks the ground once or twice more then suddenly launches into a dipping, heavy flight like a rocket out of control. It's worth waiting as five minutes will usually see a reappearance.

The green woodpecker has two interesting folk names – the 'yaffle' and the 'rain bird'. Certainly the loud scoffing call sounds like yaffling laughter. There is less agreement as to the origin of the name 'rain bird'. French and German folklore has it that the green woodpecker refused to help other birds to scoop out pools, rivers and seas at the time of the Creation. God forbade the woodpecker to drink from these sources and allowed it rainwater only. The green woodpecker, therefore, cries out for rain.

Unlikely though this story is, the green woodpecker does seem to call most often during long sunny spells. The bird also appears to call in the prickly stillness seconds before the first spots of rain. It may be that the mocking laughter sounds louder in these atmospheric conditions. When I first started to study the wildlife of the Bristol Downs, there was a green woodpecker in Black Rock Gully which laughed loudly some minutes after rain had actually started. The current green woodpeckers are more confident of their predictions.

Green woodpeckers, tormentil and harebells

SEPTEMBER

1ST **6.30 a.m.** Squirrels are tossing down portions of conker cases from high in the horse chestnuts.

The football pitches near the Gorge host a busy community of gulls and starlings this morning. One swift is flying above Black Rock Gully.

There are springy mats of tormentil in the short turf and harebells are flowering in the dry meadow grass. Clinging to one strand of grass and rocking in the breeze is a tiny male common blue butterfly the size of my little fingernail. Eyebright is flowering on this rocky bank – an alert, aptly named flower once supposed to sharpen the eyesight of linnets – though it's hard to see how anyone could arrive at that conclusion.

4TH **6.45 a.m.** Running this morning, I am overtaken by a kestrel, flying just above the ground to my right. I speed up and together we race across the football pitches and towards the Sea Walls. The kestrel soars upwards and circles the Gorge.

5TH This rock-rose has a red back to its yellow petals: rock-roses seem to darken in colour throughout the year.

8TH Musk thistles, growing in thick clumps on the Dumps, attract bees and seem to drug them. I have put a chalk mark on one bee and will try to find the bee again later.

The blackberries are at their best today.

9TH The chalked bee is still on the same thistle.

At the top of a bare stem of plantain near the thistle there are hundreds of minute silver-grey eggs.

11TH The eggs have gone and the top of the stem is thinner and black. Chalked bee still on same thistle.

12TH **7.30 a.m.** Chalked bee still in place.

A heron is flying over the Downs towards Southmead.

13TH Chalked bee gone. Huge garden cross spiders' webs are slung from thistle to thistle.

The hawthorns are thick with berries which from a distance look like scarlet blossom.

14TH Near Observatory Hill – a small heart carved into the bark of this sycamore and four ladybirds inside the heart, making it red.

SEPTEMBER

15TH This morning smells like autumn. Some of the horse chestnut leaves are toast-brown. The robins are singing again. Here are three young jackdaws and one has a large clod of cut grass stuck to his feet like a boot.

16TH One autumn lady's tresses orchid in the dry grass. It is about 7 cm high and neatly plaited.

Elderberries look navy blue in the sunshine.

23RD Calm after the gales last night. Conkers and cases are littering the ground under the chestnuts.

Ash-keys are golden brown.

There are 'sticky buds' already on the end of the horse chestnut branches.

26TH On this harebell is a white crab spider, its legs and body bent into a perfect imitation of a seedcase. A lethal hunter and master of disguise, this spider will slowly change colour to match its surroundings.

Conkers are crunchy underfoot – it's unpleasant, like treading on snails.

The paths under the beeches in the Promenade are dark brown with nuts and cases.

30TH It sounds as though a robin is singing in every hawthorn this morning.

Two young goldfinches are plucking seeds from a dandelion and dissecting a rose-hip.

Holly berries are orange. Rose-hips are coral-pink and on this bush, one rose remains.

The bushes are a wonderland of cobwebs and on this dead tree the webs are in layers from the lowest to the highest branch – ghostly foliage.

At the bottom of a copper beech there are four brussels sprout plants gone to seed.

Horse chestnuts, squirrel and magpie

HORSE CHESTNUTS

The whole of Durdham Down is enclosed by horse chestnuts, the most generous of trees, bearing spectacular spring flowers and the rich autumn conker harvest. There is always something going on with a horse chestnut – it's a dynamic, rewarding tree to watch.

Those large brown terminal buds are shining before Christmas, the stickiness being a resin to stop invading insects. Should any buds be blown off by gales, we may have an opportunity to undertake a strange experiment recommended by Geoffrey Grigson '. . . soak horse chestnut buds and twigs in water. Shine a torch through the water and it will glow with a blue luminescence.'*

'After New Year, it's a matter of which bud will open first? And then, which tree will be the first to leaf? Though a particularly precipitate horse chestnut near the White Tree roundabout is usually the victor. Next, it's which tree will offer the first white blossoms and which of the red hybrid trees will be the first. The red and white display along Saville Road is breathtaking.

Spring gales bring down candles of blossom and large, umbrella-like leaves. This is our chance to smell the blossoms and study their structure. Flowers open from the bottom of the spike and resemble a corsage of waxy, tropical orchids. The white blossoms have yellow marks on them and it's intriguing to notice the way these become red as the flower ages.

The fruits gradually swell and actual conker prospecting starts in August. Conkers now are fool's gold because the cases brought down by winds contain disappointingly white balls.

By late September, the harvest is ready and the trees endure their annual harassment. It's an unnecessary attack because the ripest harvest is on the ground.

A love of these mahogany treasures unites us all. I've met grandfathers foraging for their grandchildren (or so they said). Afterwards they sat down on a bench and compared booty. I watched a father and toddler son out at dawn, filling an enormous dustbin bag with the night's windfalls and later, a smart lady with a briefcase asked me to direct her to

---

* Grigson, *The Shell Guide to Trees and Shrubs*, (Phoenix House 1958).

the conkers. One golden afternoon, too, a red motorcycle roared into Westbury Park. The rider pulled off his crash helmet, turned it upside down and filled it with conkers.

But even when the conkers are a floury powder over the roads, these trees have more to offer. Giant, rusty leaves fall in layers and it's good to walk among these and admire their size and colour. After the fall of the leaves – the 'sticky buds' again – and keep an eye *under* these trees for the ungathered conkers which remain intact and begin to sprout in the spring.

Note The areas around the horse chestnuts are an ideal place to search for squirrels. Loved as endearing or loathed as killers of trees, there's some fascination in the meaning of their name – squirrel means 'shadow tail' – and in their impossible lightness and speed.

OCTOBER

1ST 7.30 a.m. There are a lot of fairy rings in the turf around the football pitches and a male and a female mallard duck in the grass by the Sea Walls.

6TH 7.00 a.m. Two low-flying swans head over the Granny Downs towards Redland.
11.00 a.m. It's hot and here's a comma butterfly, clinging to an ivy flower, wings wide open to the sun.

This hazel twig has eight small snails on it, all shining silver in the sun like pussy willow.

The mistletoe clusters have small green berries.

9TH The lime trees are crowned with gold and the Granny Downs are scattered with scarlet maple leaves.

The bark of this plane tree is a mosaic of green, grey, brown and yellow.

Most of the blackberries are mouldy.

11TH There is an ever-widening circle of fallen leaves under the limes and four magpies are patrolling these golden shadows. A plump garden cross spider is bouncing from a long thread hooked to the buddleia.

12TH 7.00 a.m. I pass five rooks on the grass near Black Rock Gully: three young and their parents. One of the young has almost completely white wings. A kestrel lands on a nearby hawthorn. At once, the rooks take to the air and mob the kestrel, making him leave his bush, flying above him and forcing him down. Almost on the grass, the kestrel turns, squawks and pecks. This battle continues for many minutes until the kestrel flies away over the Gorge. Was the rooks' ferocity because one of the young is a partial albino? Albinos are always vulnerable.

14TH Still a few short-stemmed harebells in the turf. I kneel to look at a bumble-bee, wondering if it is dead. The bee takes off loudly and crash-lands a few metres away. A peacock butterfly passes us.

I can smell the ivy flowers: no wonder the wasps are attracted.

A colony of rusty-brown broomrape under this hawthorn and, above it, a tangle of ivy and fluffy white clematis plumes. Even higher up – cascades of powder-pink spindle

Kestrel

berries. These berries are strange both in shape and in their matt intensity. Most berries are shiny.

15TH Elm leaves turn to gold after they have fallen: they tend to stay yellow and green on the tree.

The maples have shed their red leaves and the spring-like pale yellow and green layers remain, awaiting their turn to redden and fall.

Earthballs in the grass are like brown birds' eggs.

The conkers are being ground to floury white powder by the cars.

20TH Gales this morning and the gulls swoop and curve like whitebeam leaves on the wind. Fallen leaves have been dispersed to a wider area and now there are golden shadows around the hawthorns.

Silver birch leaves are beginning to turn yellow.

The black and red berries of the wayfaring trees look like counters for a children's game.

21ST Frost last night and the veins of the fallen beech leaves are white.

23RD Dewy and warm but there's frost-like gossamer all over the grass.

25TH I follow a couple walking through Fairyland and a hamster-like creature is apparently following them. It's a weasel.

The squirrels are noisy as they search the dead leaves under a beech.

There's a salmon-breasted nuthatch on one of the outer branches of this ash.

As I approach the Dumps, five pigeons fly off with a sound like applause.

26TH Ribena-coloured amethyst deceiver fungi are well camouflaged among the fallen beech leaves.

Under a holm oak, a colony of eight shaggy parasol mushrooms - one is 17 cm across. Close by, the bilious-yellow heads of death cap, the most deadly fungus known.

28TH Two pied wagtails scuttle past the Water Tower, taking off into skipping flight and dropping down to earth with rocket-like speed. They start to rock and walk immediately they touch the earth.

The green woodpecker is attacking the worm-casts.

A congregation of tits is passing from the silver birch to the yew. The long-tailed tits lead, followed by blue tits, great tits and goldfinches.

29TH There's a patch of small-flowered crane's-bill by Westbury Road: its purple flowers are smaller than the bud of the daisy next to it.

31ST One rock-rose in Black Rock Gully. These roses rarely open fully in the autumn: they stay in half-blossom like little yellow bonnets, their seedcases like oriental lanterns.

PIED WAGTAILS AND THE SEVEN SISTERS

High-pitched calls and a wavy flight announce the arrival of a pair of pied wagtails to the turf around the Seven Sisters. These lively black and white birds can often be seen here, along the pavements of Westbury Road or scuttling between parked cars at the Water Tower.

Apart from roosting, pied wagtails are birds of the ground and air; they are not usually to be found in the trees of the Downs. I've only once observed a pair of these birds in a tree – in the lowest branches of a horse chestnut near the Water Tower. The female wagtail followed the male uneasily along the branches, copying his footholds and the two birds completed an above-ground circuit of the tree before dropping to the pavement where they wagged and rocked with their usual clockwork vigour.

Pied wagtails rise and dip in flight like skimmed pebbles, calling all the while. They fly high and drop rapidly, skylark-fashion and it's entertaining to watch these birds start to walk and wag the very second they touch the ground.

And what of the Seven Sisters themselves, the Downs' most famous landmark? For many years, these Austrian pines numbered six – and then five. Superstition, of course, surrounds the number seven and there's something of a mystic atmosphere in the winter when the pines are white with frost or shrouded in mist. There's beauty, too, in this otherwise rather bleak area when the shimmering wonderland of cobwebs covers the turf and it's full of little paths worn by students on their way to the University from the Halls of Residence.

The turf near the Seven Sisters houses the earliest cowslips on the Downs – and the tiniest. Regularly decapitated by the mowers, these cowslips rapidly grow again as short-stemmed miniatures.

But the real magic of the Seven Sisters is in the sky above them, in the sight of the winter redwings almost falling to roost in the nearby beech, in the occasional chases and conflicts between birds and in the pre-roost flying display of a murmuration of starlings.

A heron often flies over the Seven Sisters, too, especially in the early morning – huge wings dipping slowly like an aerial boatman rowing towards Southmead.

Pied wagtails and the Seven Sisters

NOVEMBER

3RD Some trees have been stripped bare by last night's gale but the beech and silver birch are defiantly yellow against a grey sky. A jay is pecking at the ground under a hawthorn near the White Tree.

There's a small clump of buttercups by the Seven Sisters and a double rainbow over Wills Hall.

5TH Under a holm oak, nine squirrels are jumping from the ground to the branches and back again, tossing down scraps of acorns to the already messy floor.

20 metres from the White Tree roundabout, a shaggy ink cap fungus.

Shaggy ink cap fungus

6TH 7.00 a.m. The silent convoy of gulls is flying in from Avonmouth: one of the gulls is trying to fly and scratch its beak at the same time.

The kestrel is sitting under one of the wooden seats.

There's an amethyst deceiver fungus in the middle of this muddy path, kicked over and trampled: fungi seem to invite this response.

A song thrush is using one of the trim trail leap-frog trunks as an anvil. A charm of goldfinches flies between the hawthorns, surfing through the air. One greenfinch follows with a markedly heavier flight.

10TH More fungi. The revolting jew's ear fungus is on nearly every branch of this elder and there's sulphur tuft on the emerald moss of a dead tree-trunk – looking like custard-pie on a green carpet.

Among the fallen wet leaves of the oak and the ash, the shaggy-stemmed, attractively green, *verdigris agaric:* poisonous. And here are three pert and pointed liberty caps. Lovely name – hallucinogenic fungus.

12TH 8.00 a.m. A heron flies out of the fog above me and disappears back into it. Fog distorts perception of size and the bird looks enormous and prehistoric.

NOVEMBER

Two pied wagtails line up on the kerb of Westbury Road. They chatter, confer and consult, nod in agreement and then choose the most hazardous seconds to dip their way between lorries. Safely on the other side, they fly off like skimmed pebbles. The badgers have been active last night: there is evidence of much digging and snuffling and the dung pits are full. I extract a dozen black and white badger hairs from the diggings.

There is a patch of candle-snuff fungus on this decaying tree-trunk.

18TH Only a few yellow leaves remain on this birch; they look like the fading golden sparks of a firework.

Orange seeds are pushing through the pink cases of the spindle berries.

The green woodpecker looks colourful on this dismal afternoon, her rump yellow and her head startlingly red.

A lot of the fungi is disintegrating into slop.

20TH The hawthorns around the Dumps are alive with birds!

I count 22 long-tailed tits flying in a line from one bush to another, followed by a pair of bullfinches.

The green woodpecker is thrusting her head into the ground and above her, two jays fly a heavy wave-like passage between hawthorns.

There are six magpies near the Zoo.

Back on the Granny Downs, sparrows, chaffinches and goldfinches fly together. One sparrow flies up from the path, hovers like a hummingbird for a few seconds, and then lands on a seat.

A male blackbird listens intently to the mewing of the female in another hawthorn.

26TH Already there are tiny green buds on the sweet violets.

A kingfisher-blue fly disappears into one of the badger holes. I wait but it doesn't reappear.

Horse chestnut buds are shining in the sun.

Blackberries taste nice with frost on them.

29TH From the evidence of their dung pits, the badgers have been feasting on yew berries.

BADGERS

I haven't come face to face with a Downs' badger and it's unlikely that I will unless I hide near one of the setts all night. The Downs are active with people and cars until late at night and I doubt if the badgers would venture out before midnight.

However, from my study of badgers elsewhere and my frequent daytime visits to one of the setts, I've learned enough badger-lore to detect some of the details of their nightly forages.

I believe the sett I visit has been reoccupied recently and the two sett holes were enlarged to three in April – possibly indicating the presence of cubs born in February. One of these holes is the entrance and it's characteristically well-hidden. In the earth around this hole – especially after a wet night – I find the five-toed footprints of badgers and, in an area like the Downs, it's necessary to be able to distinguish these from the larger four-toed footprints of dogs!

One of the other holes is above the badgers' bedding area and this is the hole that 'steams' in frosty weather and attracts flies when it's warmer. The badgers occasionally bring their bedding above ground to air it and amidst the usual bedding material of grass, fern and leaves there are interesting items of Downs' rubbish – plastic sheeting, portions of rubber balls, half a sock. Badgers have a pleasant, musky smell but unlike the smell of fox, this doesn't hang about in the air. Airing bedding often smells of badger and so do the sett holes.

Badgers dig, scratch and snuffle. They dig to enlarge their setts and many experts believe that they also dig for the sake of it.

In the course of all this digging and scratching, badger hairs are shed: these straight, strong hairs are grey at the base and tip and dark in the middle.

Badgers scratch their claws on trees near the sett – either to sharpen their claws or to clean them of mud. The Downs' badgers do a lot of this and their main 'scratching tree' is deeply gored.

As for snuffling, this activity is responsible for little pits and exposed areas of earth and roots where the badgers have used their snouts to forage for beetle larvae, tubers of pignut, cuckoo pint corms and even bluebell bulbs. The favourite food of the badger is earthworms and the Downs have an abundance of these on wet nights. However, as both the time for foraging and suitable foraging areas are limited for these badgers, and from the evidence of their dung pits which give some indication of the nature of their food, it is likely that someone is feeding these badgers regularly and knows them at least as well as I do.

DECEMBER

1ST 7.00 a.m. Here come the gulls, and what's this? Flying regally down the middle of them is a heron. The gulls part like the sides of a cloak to let it through.

There are nine generous molehills near the White Tree roundabout.

2ND An old hawthorn holds eight clusters of mistletoe and the berries are white and fat.

I wonder why the hedgerows around some of the blackthorns smell so lovely. Probably a mixture of leaf mould, fungi and sweet violet leaves.

There are dozens of golden oak apples on the lower branches of this leaf-bare oak.

I stand in the centre of a yew canopy and wait for the birds I disturbed to come back. A pair of blackbirds return and sit silently above me. Blue tits and goldcrests weave in and out of the dark branches.

3RD What an extraordinary performance. Three magpies in a leafless ash; one on the lowest branch, one mid-way and one at the top. The one on the lowest branch hops to mid-way, the mid-way magpie hops to the top and the one at the top starts all over again at the bottom. This performance continues twice.

4TH What's this freshly-dug hole in the woods opposite the Zoo? I rub my hand around the entrance and withdraw it. My hand smells strongly of fox.

The leaves of the Turkey oak are a pale, carroty-orange.

Encouraged by my birdwatching under the yew, I stand in the darkness of a hawthorn island and wait for the birds to settle around me. I wait and wait. I give up and as I leave, at least a dozen birds fly out past me. Where were they?

There are five more molehills and thousands of worm-casts in the turf this morning.

8TH The Downs are white with frost, the daisies are crystallised and rooks are circling a frozen puddle. Two of the badger holes are steaming.

11TH An even thicker frost: the trees are white.

2.00 p.m. The frost has melted from the trees but is thick and crunchy on the grass. The sun is pastel and low and

Wren

shining through the black skeletons of the trees. Puffed up in the cold, the pigeons look enormous.
4.00 p.m. The Downs are aglow: the white grass is like crystal and the setting sun is smouldering scarlet. It's like walking in a dream.

17TH **9.15 a.m.** The grass around the Seven Sisters is full of gulls and above, the kestrel is circling, screaming and dipping.

Badger pawprints are clear in the wet, red earth.

21ST There is a green woodpecker on the Granny Downs, flying into the umbrella-like protection of a hawthorn.

22ND Above the Gorge, above the gulls, the peregrine falcon riding the wind.

There are new burgundy and green leaves on the elders, pink shoots on the tips of the elms and the sycamore buds look as though they would burst into life at the slightest encouragement.

White and pink winter heliotrope is flowering in this woodland – a clumsy flower for so sweet a scent.

24TH Yet more molehills extending towards the White Tree. As I watch, one of the hills wriggles. I watch for 30 minutes in the fading afternoon light, hoping for a glimpse of mole. More movement – the whole structure heaves and settles. Tantalising.

DECEMBER

25TH Three more molehills surrounded by frozen worm-casts.

Two wrens explode out of a nearby bramble and chase each other.

The holly and the ivy are dark and glossy and the mistletoe has escaped collection.

28TH There are 36 rooks on this ash, all sitting in pairs facing the Water Tower. Nearby, a hawthorn is topped by a shuffling crow.

I can hear the liquid song of the nuthatch and see him on the oak.

Young leaves of goosegrass form snowflake patterns under the hawthorns.

29TH Three sweet violet buds are raised above the leaves and there is a slight trace of purple on them.

A robin lands on the lowest branch of the beech above my head.

A cormorant is flying over Fairyland.

ROBINS

My love of the wildlife of the Bristol Downs started with a robin. We made our first family attempts to observe wildlife by sitting in a clump of trees near Bristol Zoo and within minutes a robin began to circle around us, flipping noiselessly from branch to branch, as curious about us as we were about it.

This mutual curiosity was sufficient to captivate and we returned to the clump and its robin. Sometimes the robin joined us after several minutes and at other times it followed us impatiently, ushering us into the clump as though extending hospitality to its territory. Ten years later and just beginning to write this book, I returned to the same clump to see if it is still possible to attract a robin there so quickly. Yes; an equally enchanting bird joined me and as it circled, I could see its beak open and close in a muted, tentative warbling.

It's possible to see and hear a robin on the Downs at any time of day and at any time of the year except the late summer when the robins temporarily abandon their territories for their moult. We have a double chance of hearing robins because both males and females sing. Robins are also among the first birds to sing in the dawn chorus and often sing on well into the evening when other birds have fallen silent.

There's a difference between the spring song of the robin, clear, sharp, intense, and the sadder, perhaps more conventionally lovely autumn melody. The robin's song seems the sweetest of all in April, when the air holds the sound and prolongs it as a shimmer for several breathtaking seconds.

Robins habitually sing from open perches on the Downs; in the spring there seems to be a robin in every hawthorn and in the winter a robin next to the berries in every holly bush. Even the scientific name of the robin refers to its song: *Erithacus rubecula melophilus* – little sweet-singing red one.

As robins make frequent boundary inspections of their territories, their movements are fairly predictable. One of the Downs' robins includes a short rock climb in his boundary inspection and another, in Fairyland, conscientiously visits both ends of a wooden seat on his rounds.

Robin, mistletoe and ivy

INTRODUCING THE WILDLIFE WALKS

There are actually 13 walks, one for each month and two for May. Over the course of the year these walks will take you to all the main areas of the Downs as well as a few you may not know very well such as Fairyland, the ash wood and the Zoo woods. The aim is to put you in the right place at the right time to see the Downs' wildlife, as well as the best landscape views.

Each walk is linked to the diary observations for the month. For a feast for the eyes try the walks very early in the morning – sunrise on the Bristol Downs is spectacular.

All the walks are circular, so you can start where you like, but we have indicated a natural start point where there is plenty of parking space.

The recommended route is represented by a green line. The arrows indicate our preferred direction for walking the route. Note which side of the road the route goes, this is usually important, especially round the Circular Road. Also check how far the route runs away from the road. Where the green line snakes about you should take time to search around a bit because this is an interesting area for wildlife.

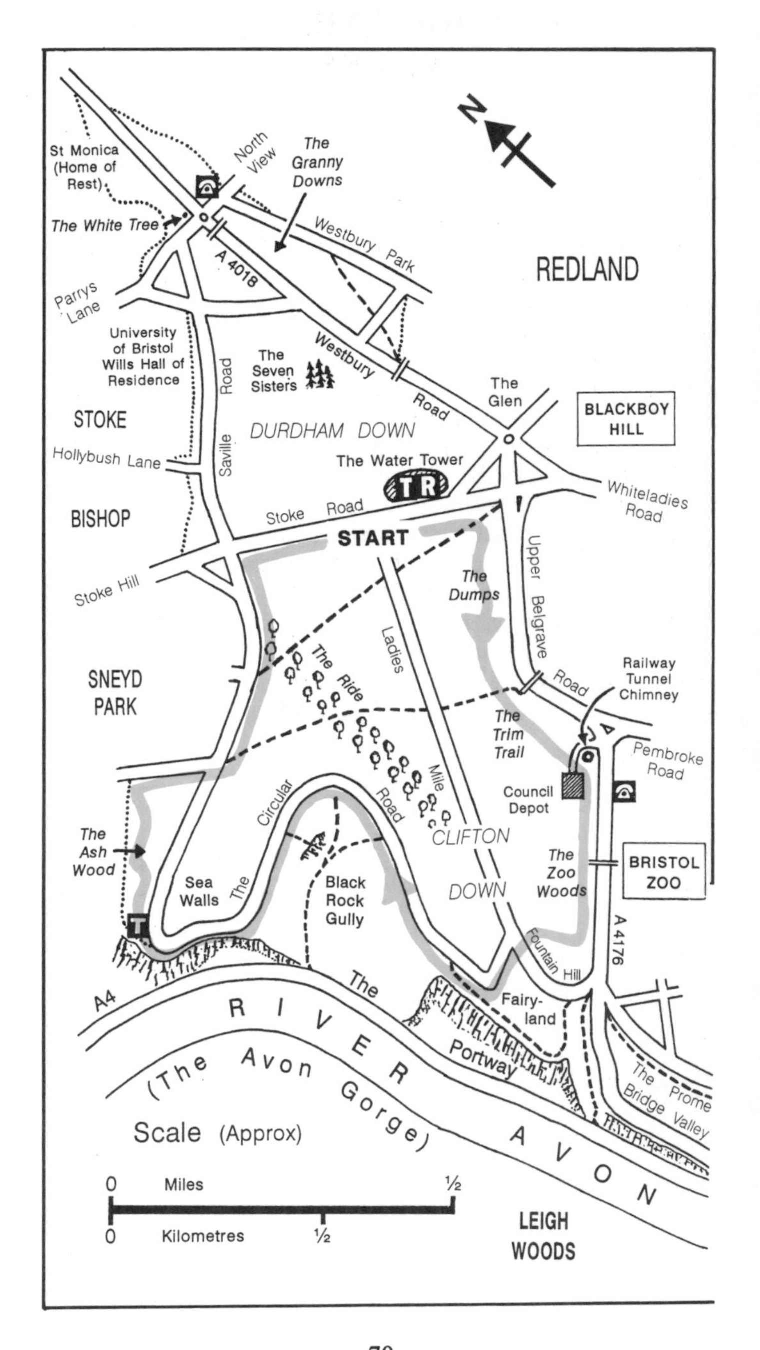
St Monica
(Home of
Rest)
North
View
The
Granny
Downs
The White Tree
Westbury Park
A 4018
REDLAND
Parrys
Lane
University
of Bristol
Wills Hall of
Residence
The
Seven
Sisters
Westbury
Road
The
Glen
BLACKBOY
HILL
STOKE
Saville
Road
DURDHAM DOWN
Hollybush Lane
The Water Tower
TR
Whiteladies
Road
BISHOP
Stoke Road
START
Stoke Hill
The
Dumps
Upper Belgrave Road
Ladies
The Ride
Railway
Tunnel
Chimney
SNEYD
PARK
The
Trim
Trail
Pembroke
Road
Mile
Council
Depot
Circular
Road
CLIFTON
DOWN
The
Ash
Wood
The
Zoo
Woods
BRISTOL
ZOO
Sea
Walls
The
Black
Rock
Gully
Fountain Hill
A 4176
T
A4
The
Portway
Fairy-
land
RIVER
(The Avon Gorge)
AVON
The
Bridge Valley
The
Prome
Scale (Approx)
0
Miles
½
0
Kilometres
½
LEIGH
WOODS

JANUARY

The New Year Bird Walk

Most of the action this month is in the air: take your binoculars.

Look out for:

robins
blackbirds
mistle thrushes
redwings
jackdaws
pied wagtails
long-tailed tits
blue tits
green woodpeckers
magpies

Wildlife mission for children

Look out for old birds' nests – you can spot them fairly easily in the leafless trees and bushes.

Distance:

About 2¾ miles (4½ km). Allow 1¾ hours.

MAP KEY

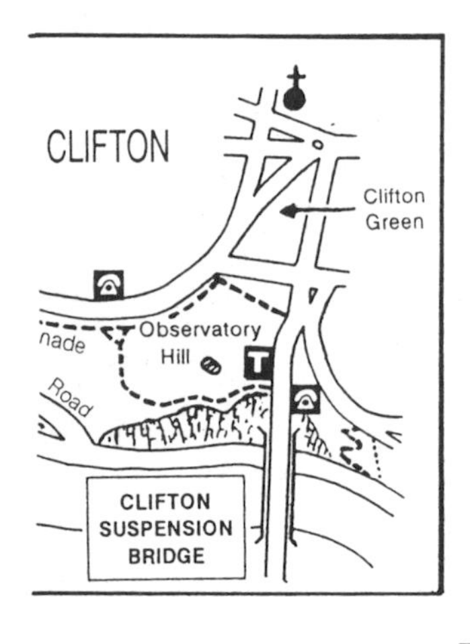

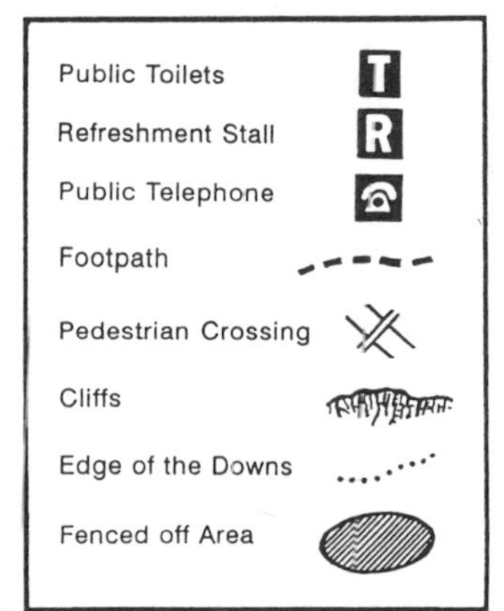

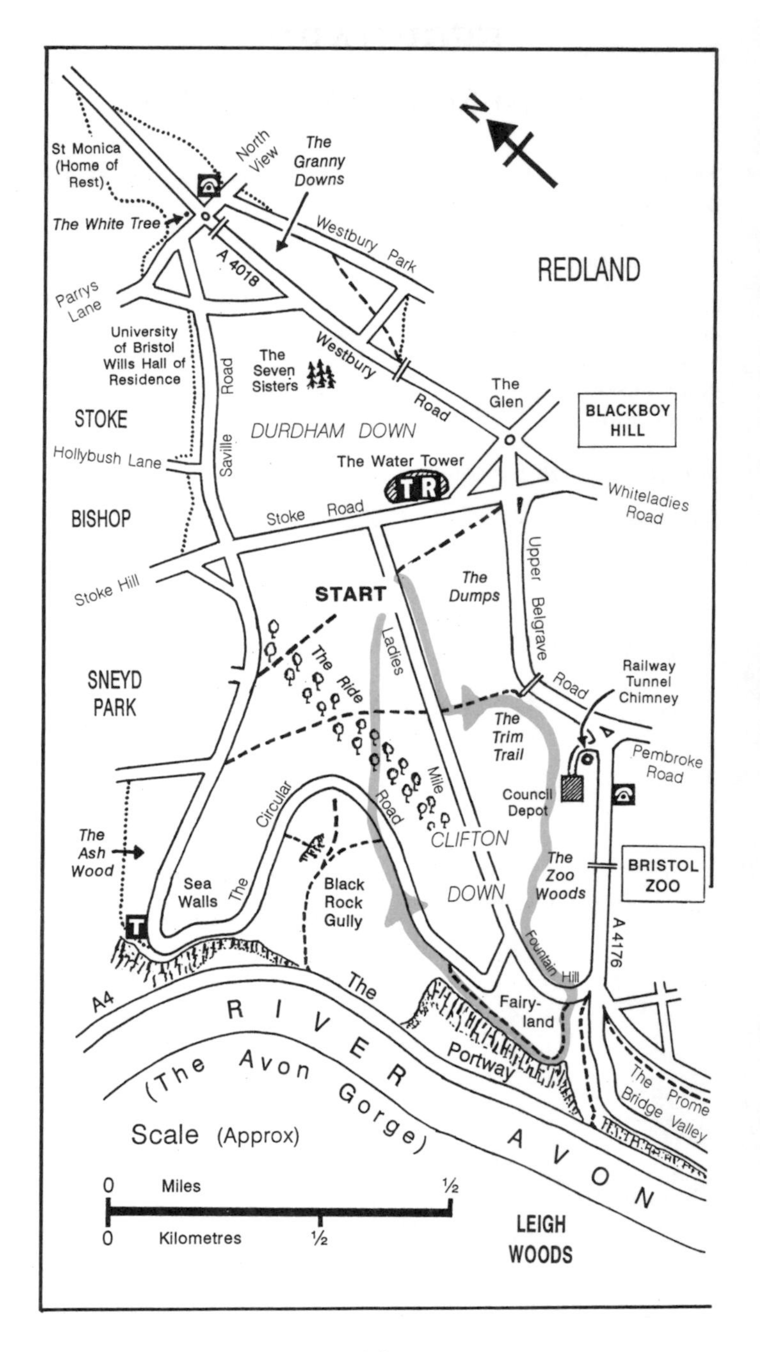
St Monica (Home of Rest)
North View
The Granny Downs
The White Tree
Westbury Park
A 4018
REDLAND
Parrys Lane
University of Bristol Wills Hall of Residence
The Seven Sisters
Westbury Road
The Glen
BLACKBOY HILL
STOKE
DURDHAM DOWN
Saville Road
Hollybush Lane
The Water Tower
TR
Whiteladies Road
BISHOP
Stoke Road
Stoke Hill
START
The Dumps
Upper Belgrave Road
Ladies Mile Road
The Ride
SNEYD PARK
Railway Tunnel Chimney
The Trim Trail
Pembroke Road
Council Depot
The Circular Road
CLIFTON DOWN
The Ash Wood
The Zoo Woods
BRISTOL ZOO
Sea Walls
Black Rock Gully
Fountain Hill
A 4176
T
A4
The Portway
Fairy-land
RIVER AVON
(The Avon Gorge)
The Bridge Valley Prome
Scale (Approx)
0 Miles ½
0 Kilometres ½
LEIGH WOODS

FEBRUARY

The First Signs of Spring Walk

There's more to look at than you think this month. It's a treasure hunt.

Look out for:

catkins
wild clematis leaves
elm roses
dog's mercury
cuckoo pint leaves
barren strawberry flowers
sweet violets
yew flowers
celandines

Wildlife mission for children

Listen to the bird song. Do big birds always have big songs or are the small birds the loudest singers?

Distance:

About $1\frac{3}{4}$ miles (3 km). Allow $1\frac{1}{4}$ hours.

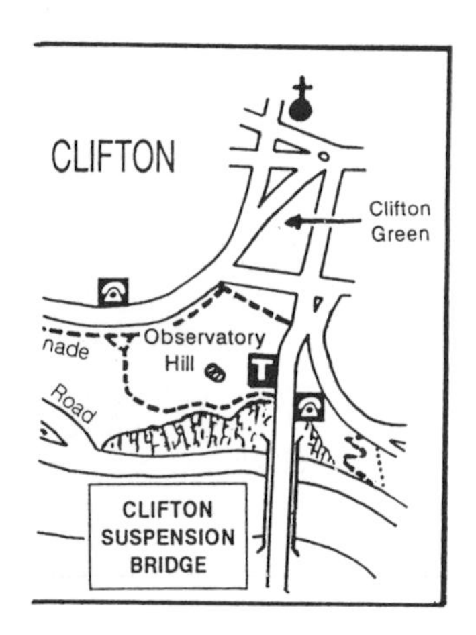

MAP KEY

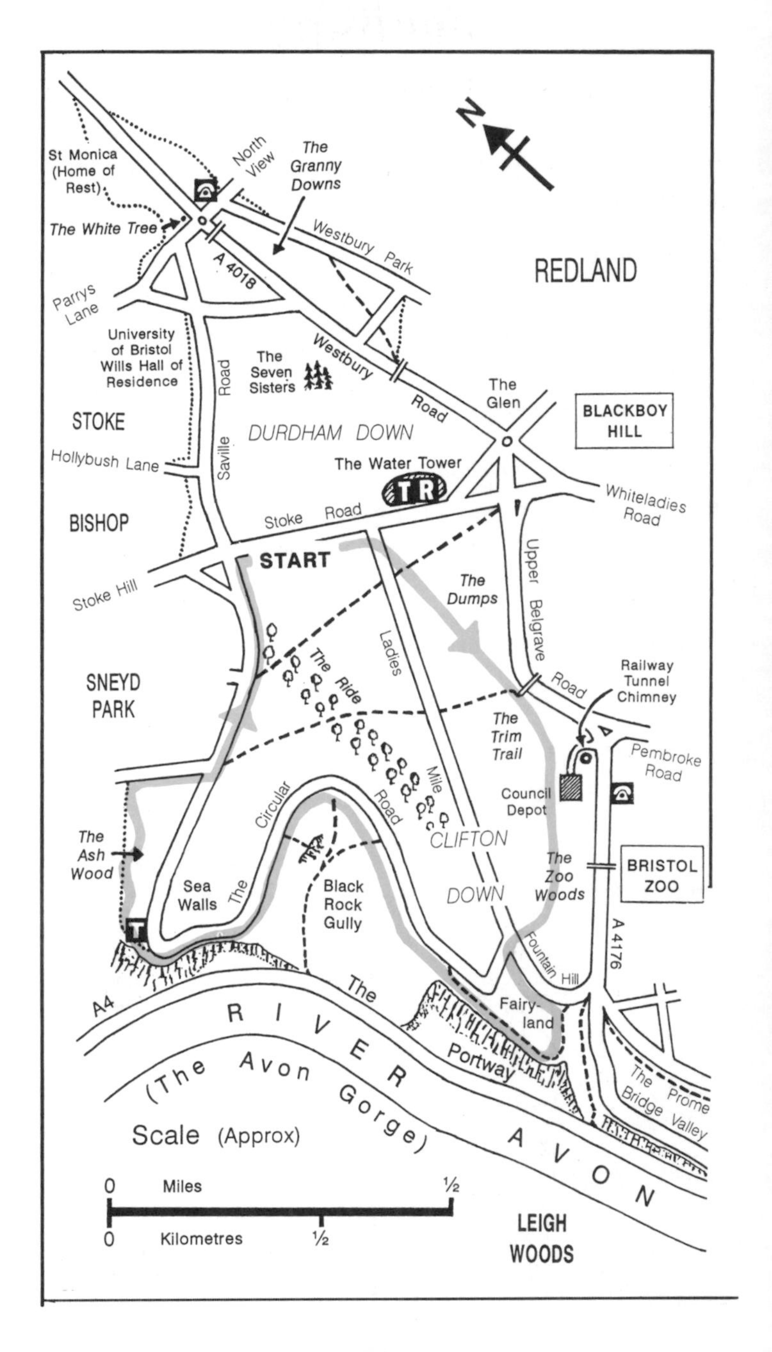

St Monica (Home of Rest)
North View
The Granny Downs
The White Tree
Westbury Park
A 4018
REDLAND
Parrys Lane
University of Bristol Wills Hall of Residence
The Seven Sisters
Westbury Road
The Glen
BLACKBOY HILL
STOKE
Saville Road
DURDHAM DOWN
Hollybush Lane
The Water Tower
TR
Whiteladies Road
BISHOP
Stoke Road
START
Stoke Hill
The Dumps
Upper Belgrave Road
SNEYD PARK
The Ride
Ladies Mile
Railway Tunnel Chimney
The Trim Trail
Pembroke Road
Council Depot
The Circular Road
CLIFTON DOWN
The Ash Wood
The Zoo Woods
BRISTOL ZOO
Sea Walls
Black Rock Gully
T
A 4176
Fountain Hill
A4
The Portway
Fairy-land
RIVER
(The Avon Gorge)
The Bridge Valley Prome
AVON
Scale (Approx)
0 Miles ½
0 Kilometres ½
LEIGH WOODS

MARCH

The Violet Walk

An exciting walk – spring is here!

Look out for:

sweet violets and dog violets
primroses
Buxbaum's speedwell
wallflowers

blackthorn blossom
wayfaring tree flowers
new leaves on limes, horse chestnuts, silver birches, sycamore
goat willow

kestrels

brimstone butterflies
bumble-bees

Wildlife mission for children

Bud watch. How many different buds can you find on plants and on the trees?

Distance:

About 3 miles (5 km). Allow 2 hours.

MAP KEY

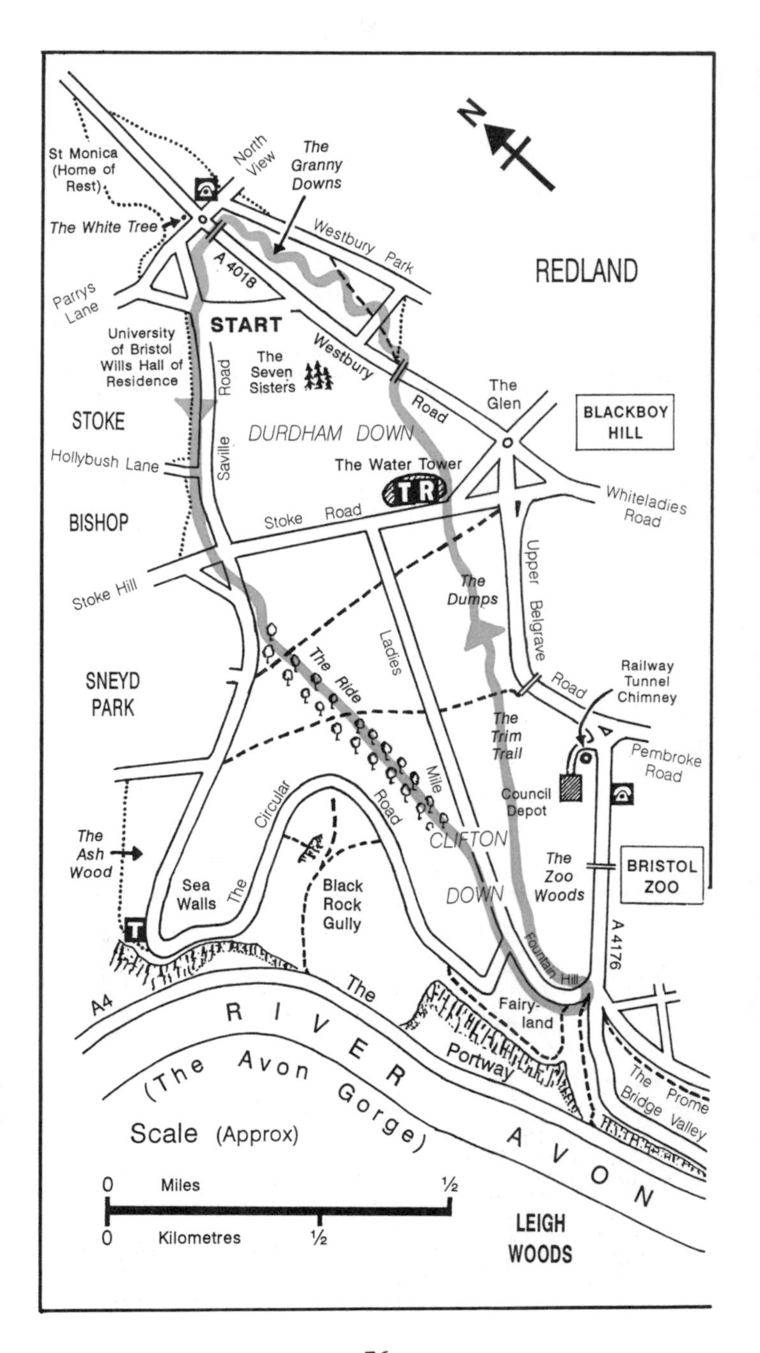
N
St Monica
(Home of
Rest)
The White Tree
North
View
The
Granny
Downs
Westbury Park
REDLAND
A 4018
Parrys
Lane
START
University
of Bristol
Wills Hall of
Residence
Westbury
Road
The
Seven
Sisters
The
Glen
BLACKBOY
HILL
STOKE
Road
Saville
DURDHAM DOWN
Hollybush Lane
The Water Tower
TR
Whiteladies
Road
BISHOP
Stoke Road
Upper
Belgrave
Road
Stoke Hill
The
Dumps
Ladies
Mile
SNEYD
PARK
The Ride
Railway
Tunnel
Chimney
The
Trim
Trail
Pembroke
Road
Council
Depot
The
Ash
Wood
Circular
Road
The
CLIFTON
DOWN
The
Zoo
Woods
BRISTOL
ZOO
Sea
Walls
Black
Rock
Gully
Fountain Hill
A 4176
T
A4
The
Portway
Fairy-
land
RIVER AVON
(The Avon Gorge)
The
Bridge Valley
The Prome
Scale (Approx)
0
Miles
½
0
Kilometres
½
LEIGH
WOODS

APRIL

The Celandine Walk

A romantic walk with a few surprises.

Look out for:

celandines
sweet violets and dog violets
daisies
buttercups
spring cinquefoil
germander speedwell
Buxbaum's speedwell
wood anemones
hawthorn leaves

ladybirds

nesting birds – especially blackbirds, great tits and long-tailed tits

St. George's mushroom (end of the month)

Wildlife mission for children

Daisy watch: who can find the reddest daisy?
Rain watch: What do flowers and birds do when it rains?

Distance:

About 3 miles (5 km). Allow 2 hours.

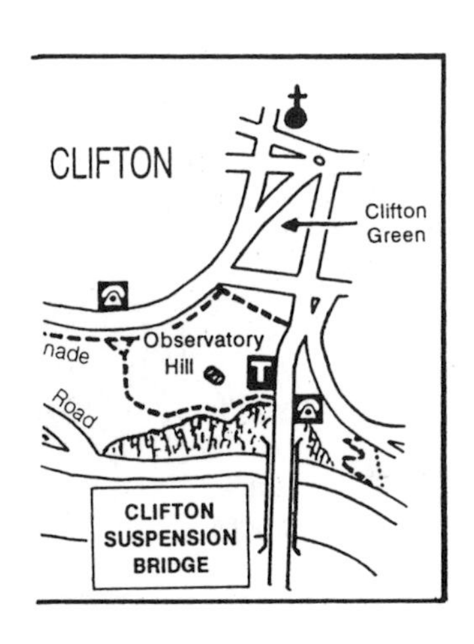

MAP KEY

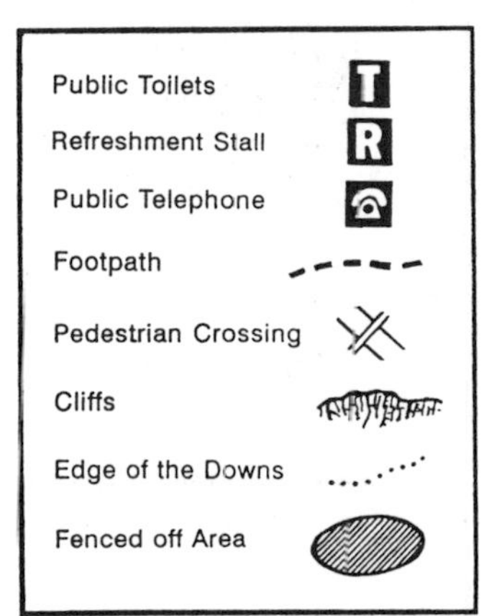

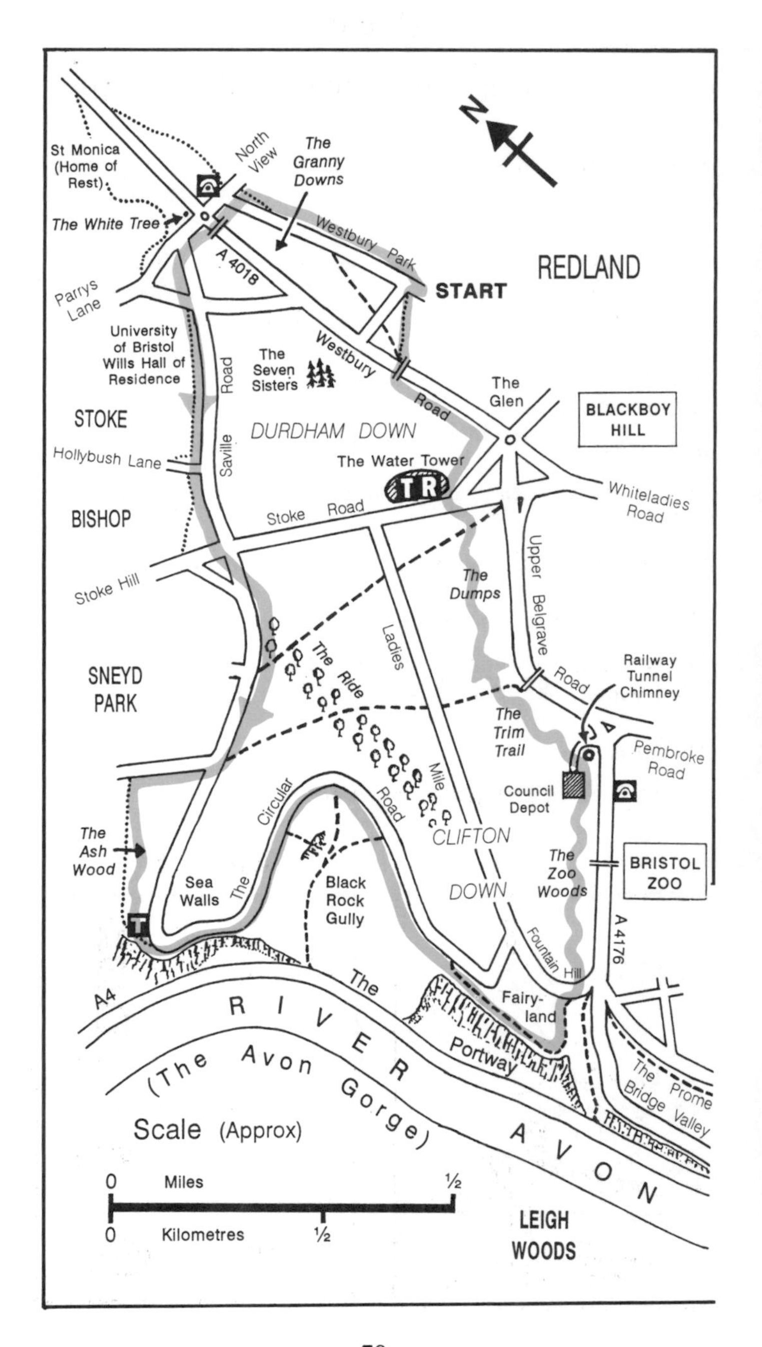
St Monica (Home of Rest)
The White Tree
North View
The Granny Downs
Westbury Park
A 4018
START
REDLAND
Parrys Lane
University of Bristol Wills Hall of Residence
The Seven Sisters
Westbury Road
The Glen
BLACKBOY HILL
STOKE
Saville Road
DURDHAM DOWN
Hollybush Lane
The Water Tower
TR
Whiteladies Road
BISHOP
Stoke Road
Stoke Hill
The Dumps
Upper Belgrave Road
Ladies Mile
The Ride
SNEYD PARK
Railway Tunnel Chimney
The Trim Trail
Pembroke Road
Council Depot
Circular Road
The Circular Road
CLIFTON DOWN
The Ash Wood
Sea Walls
Black Rock Gully
The Zoo Woods
BRISTOL ZOO
T
Fountain Hill
A 4176
A4
The Portway
Fairy-land
RIVER AVON
(The Avon Gorge)
The Promenade
Bridge Valley
Scale (Approx)
0 Miles ½
0 Kilometres ½
LEIGH WOODS

MAY

The Chestnut Spires Walk (Early May)

There's almost too much to see now, so there are two walks for May. Watch out for the swifts – due back in the first week in May.

Look out for:

horse chestnut spires
whitebeam flowers
wayfaring tree blossom
dog violets
buttercups
cuckoo pint
cowslips
cow parsley
look over to Leigh Woods for the colour of the new leaves

swifts
nesting and feeding birds

common blue butterflies

Wildlife mission for children

Bird watch. How many different birds can you see in 30 minutes? Can you remember what each was doing?

Distance:

About 4 miles ($6\frac{1}{2}$ km). Allow $2\frac{3}{4}$ hours.

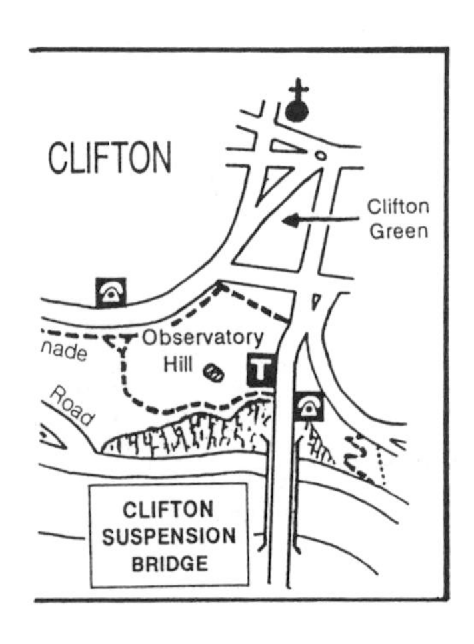

MAP KEY

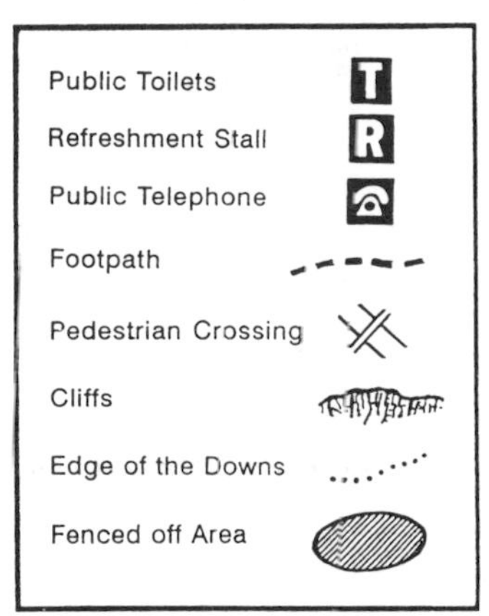

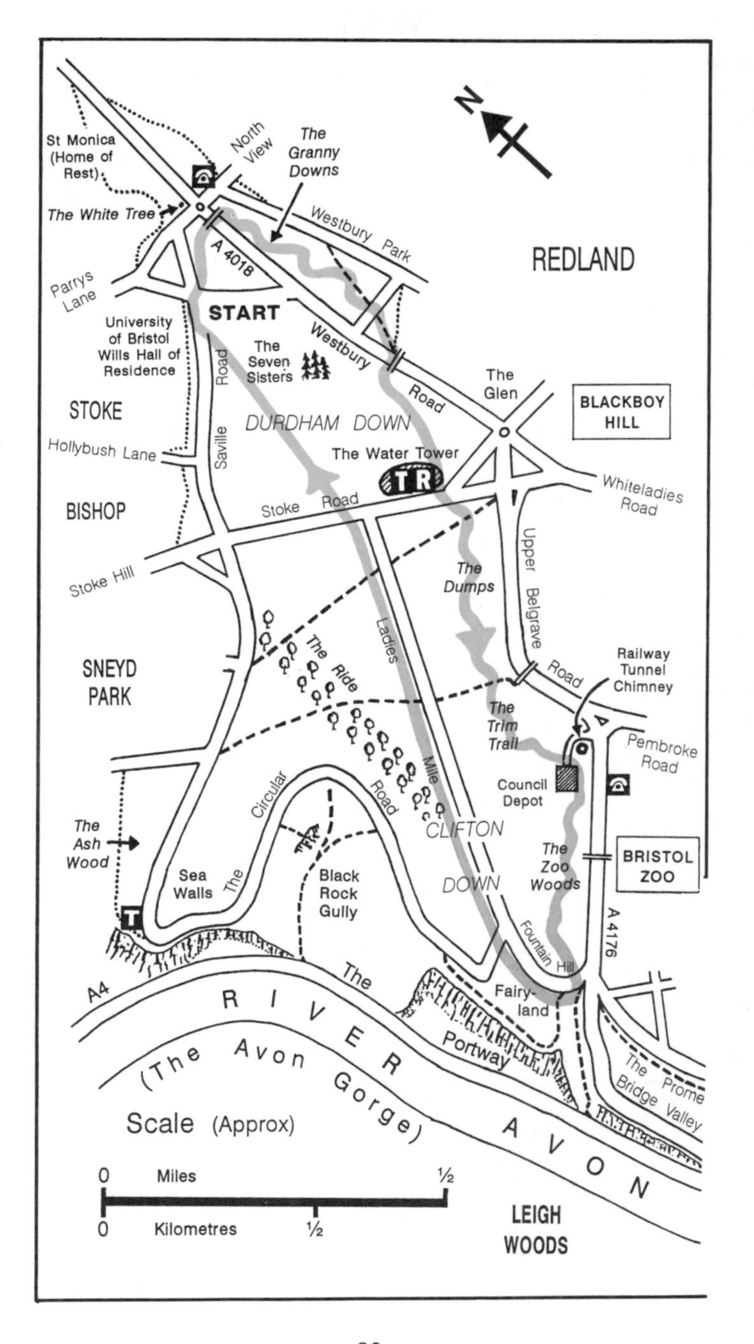
N
St Monica
(Home of
Rest)
North
View
The
Granny
Downs
The White Tree
Westbury Park
REDLAND
A 4018
Parrys
Lane
START
University
of Bristol
Wills Hall of
Residence
Westbury
Road
The
Seven
Sisters
The
Glen
BLACKBOY
HILL
STOKE
Saville
Road
DURDHAM DOWN
Hollybush Lane
The Water Tower
T R
Whiteladies
Road
BISHOP
Stoke Road
Stoke Hill
Upper Belgrave Road
The
Dumps
The Ride
Ladies
Mile
SNEYD
PARK
Railway
Tunnel
Chimney
The
Trim
Trail
Pembroke
Road
Council
Depot
The Circular Road
The
Ash
Wood
CLIFTON
DOWN
The
Zoo
Woods
BRISTOL
ZOO
Sea
Walls
Black
Rock
Gully
Fountain Hill
A 4176
T
A4
The
Portway
Fairy-
land
RIVER
(The Avon Gorge)
AVON
The Promenade
Bridge Valley
Scale (Approx)
0 Miles ½
0 Kilometres ½
LEIGH
WOODS

MAY

The May Blossom Walk (Late May)

The most classically lovely walk of all . . . and the most fragrant.

Look out for:

hawthorn (May) blossom
elm seeds
buttercups
dandelions
daisies

germander speedwell
bluebells
cowslips
salad burnet

swifts
chiffchaffs
willow warblers
blackcaps
greenfinches
peregrine falcons

orange tip butterflies

Wildlife mission for children

Flower watch. Do you know the name of that flower? Make up a name for it and this will remind you what it looked like when you try to find out what it is.

Distance:

About 2¾ miles (4½ km). Allow 1¾ hours.

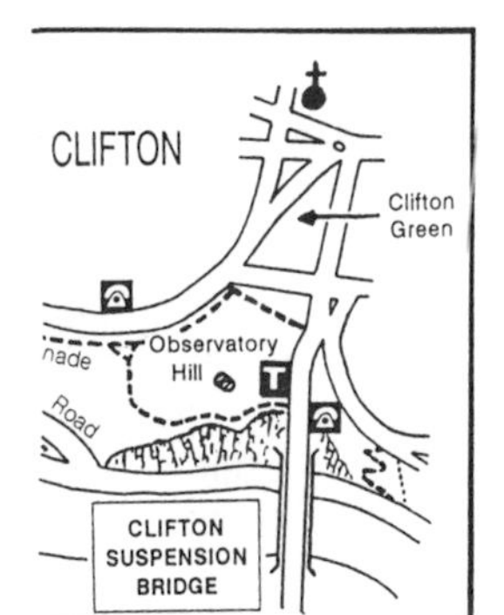

MAP KEY

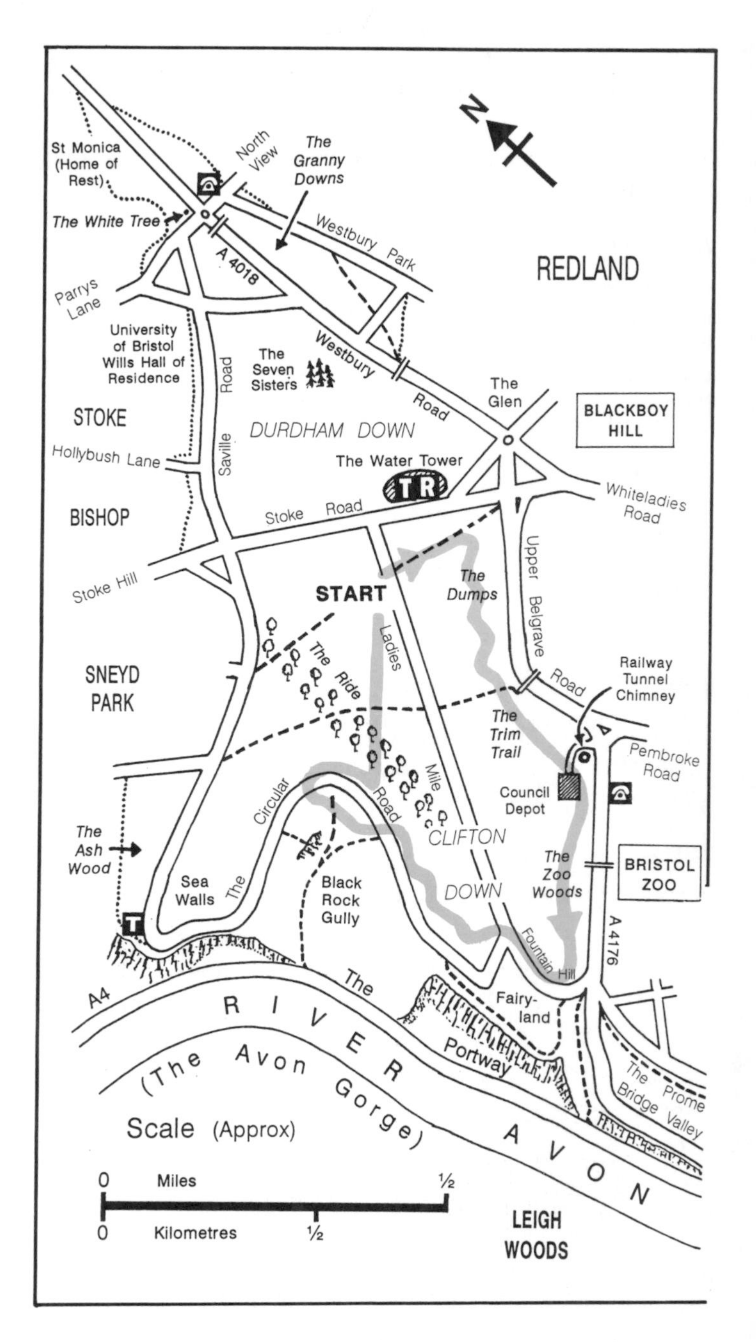
N
St Monica (Home of Rest)
North View
The Granny Downs
The White Tree
Westbury Park
REDLAND
A 4018
Parrys Lane
University of Bristol Wills Hall of Residence
The Seven Sisters
Westbury Road
The Glen
BLACKBOY HILL
STOKE
Saville Road
DURDHAM DOWN
Hollybush Lane
The Water Tower
TR
Whiteladies Road
BISHOP
Stoke Road
Upper Belgrave Road
Stoke Hill
START
The Dumps
SNEYD PARK
The Ride
Ladies Mile
Railway Tunnel Chimney
The Trim Trail
Pembroke Road
Council Depot
The Circular Road
CLIFTON DOWN
The Ash Wood
The Zoo Woods
BRISTOL ZOO
Sea Walls
Black Rock Gully
Fountain Hill
A 4176
T
A4
The Portway
Fairy-land
RIVER AVON
(The Avon Gorge)
The Bridge Valley Prome
Scale (Approx)
0 Miles ½
0 Kilometres ½
LEIGH WOODS

JUNE

The Meadow Walk

This walk will introduce you to meadow flowers you may never have seen before.

Look out for:

yellow rattle
bird's-foot-trefoil
rock-roses
dog roses

elder flowers
dropwort
ox-eye daisies

young robins and starlings

common blue butterflies

Wildlife mission for children

Go on a wondering walk. Wonder about the colour of the flowers, the names of the birds, whether trees go to sleep, the number of colours on a butterfly's wing . . .

Distance:

About 2 miles ($3\frac{1}{2}$ km). Allow $1\frac{1}{4}$ hours.

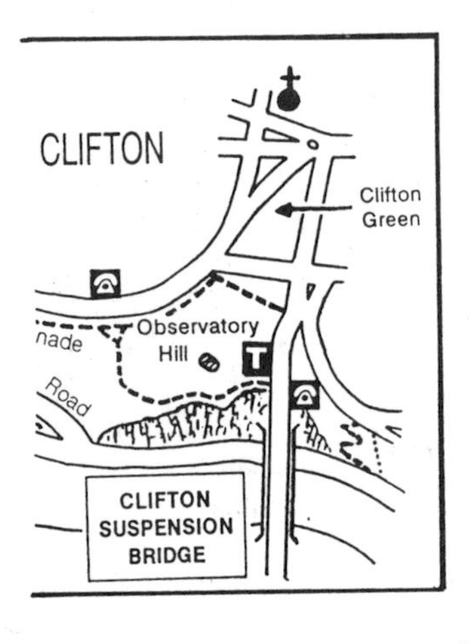

MAP KEY

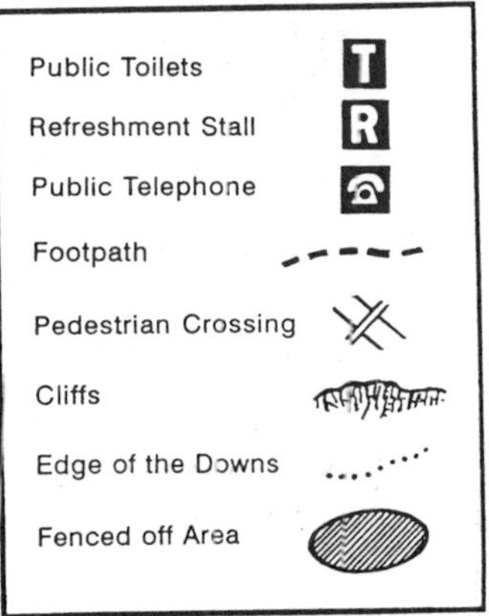

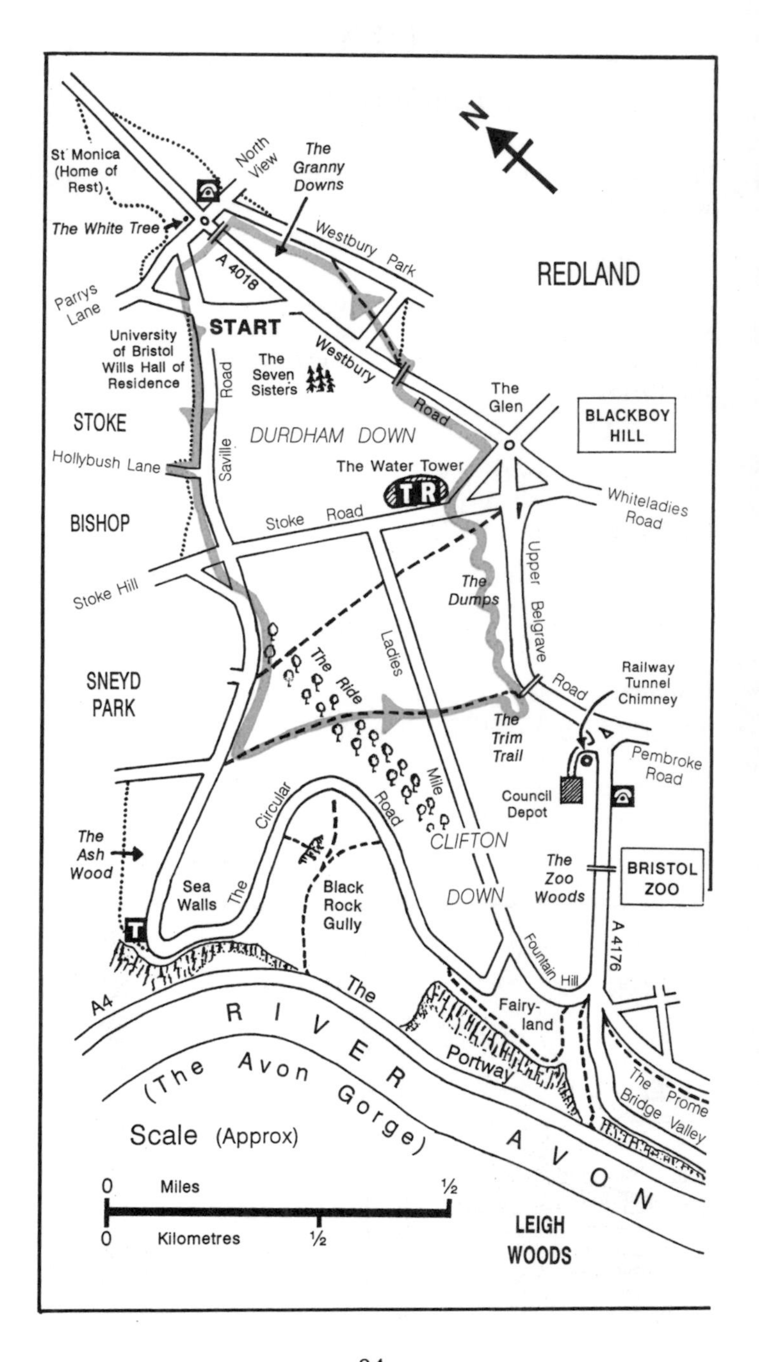

St Monica (Home of Rest)
North View
The Granny Downs
The White Tree
Westbury Park
A 4018
REDLAND
Parrys Lane
START
University of Bristol Wills Hall of Residence
The Seven Sisters
Westbury Road
The Glen
BLACKBOY HILL
STOKE
Saville Road
DURDHAM DOWN
Hollybush Lane
The Water Tower
TR
Whiteladies Road
BISHOP
Stoke Road
Stoke Hill
The Dumps
Upper Belgrave Road
SNEYD PARK
The Ride
Ladies Mile
Railway Tunnel Chimney
The Trim Trail
Pembroke Road
Council Depot
The Circular Road
CLIFTON DOWN
The Ash Wood
The Zoo Woods
BRISTOL ZOO
Sea Walls
Black Rock Gully
T
A 4176
Fountain Hill
A4
The Portway
Fairy-land
The Bridge Valley
RIVER AVON
(The Avon Gorge)
Scale (Approx)
0 Miles ½
0 Kilometres ½
LEIGH WOODS

JULY

The Lime (linden) Blossom Walk

On this sweet-smelling walk, you'll be entertained by the family behaviour of magpies, starlings, rooks and jackdaws. Look out for the peregrine falcons, too.

Look out for:

lime blossom
meadow crane's-bill
musk thistle
bramble blossom
harebells
rosebay willowherb
lady's bedstraw
crow garlic

meadow brown butterflies
marbled white butterflies

magpie families
goldfinch families
peregrine falcons

Wildlife mission for children

Look more closely . . . at flowers, trees, insects. What details can you see that you've never noticed before?

Distance:

About 2½ miles (4 km). Allow 1¾ hours.

MAP KEY

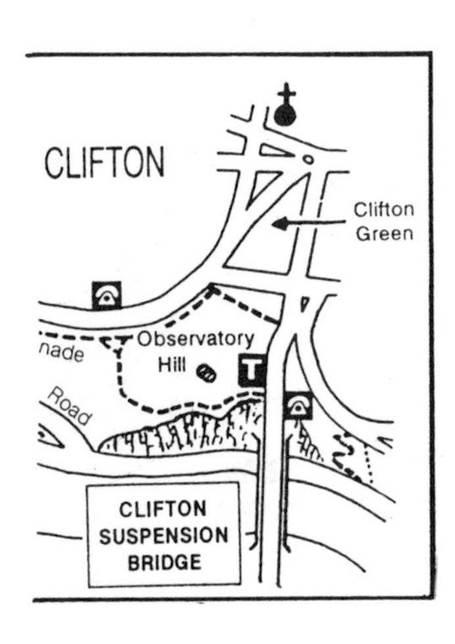

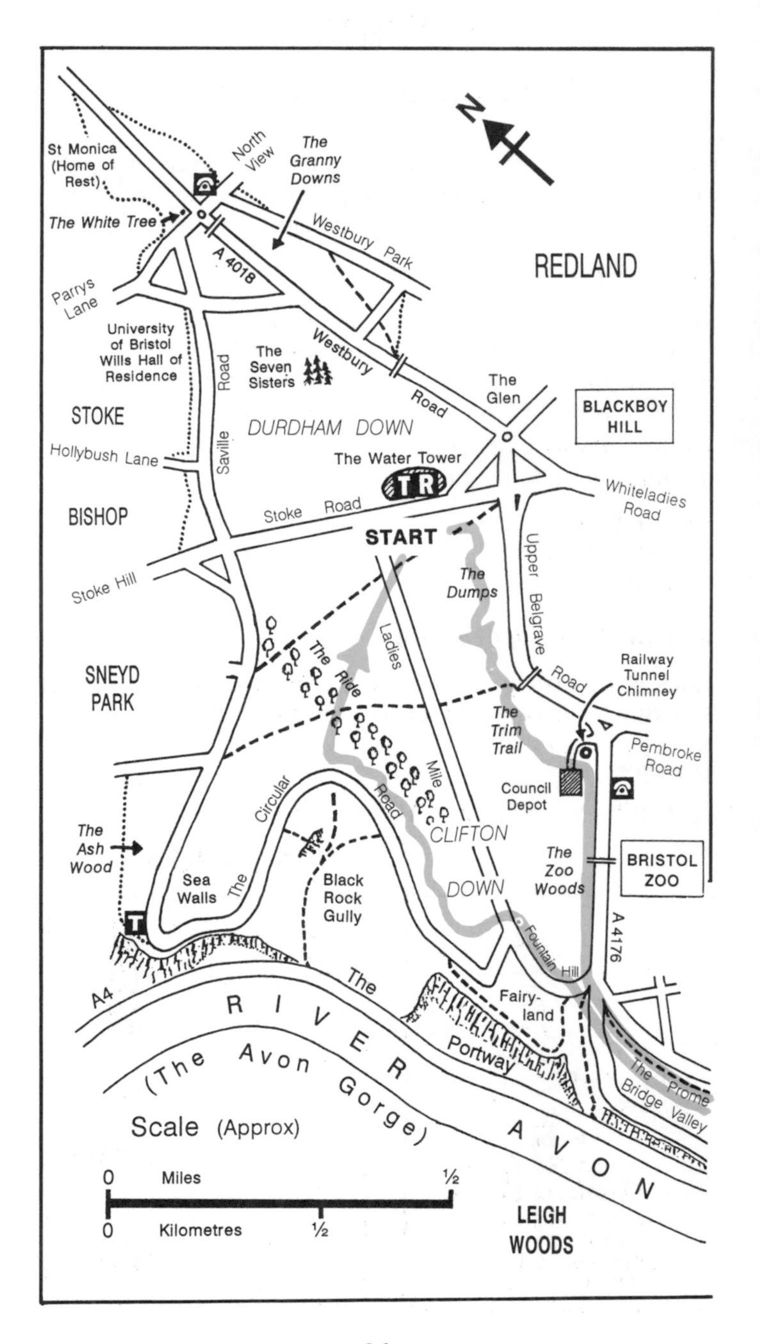
N
St Monica (Home of Rest)
North View
The Granny Downs
The White Tree
Westbury Park
A 4018
REDLAND
Parrys Lane
University of Bristol Wills Hall of Residence
The Seven Sisters
Westbury Road
The Glen
BLACKBOY HILL
STOKE
Saville Road
DURDHAM DOWN
Hollybush Lane
The Water Tower
Whiteladies Road
BISHOP
Stoke Road
START
Upper Belgrave Road
Stoke Hill
The Dumps
Ladies Mile Road
The Ride
SNEYD PARK
Railway Tunnel Chimney
The Trim Trail
Pembroke Road
Council Depot
The Circular Road
The Ash Wood
CLIFTON DOWN
The Zoo Woods
BRISTOL ZOO
Sea Walls
Black Rock Gully
Fountain Hill
A 4176
Fairy-land
A4
The Portway
RIVER
(The Avon Gorge)
The Bridge Valley
The Prome
AVON
Scale (Approx)
0 Miles ½
0 Kilometres ½
LEIGH WOODS

AUGUST

The Butterfly Walk

Feel the change: summer brightness, autumn tints.

Look out for:

butterflies, including:
common blue
marbled white
comma
small white
small tortoiseshell
six-spot burnet moth
peacock
red admiral
speckled wood
brimstone
meadow brown

knapweed
harebells
wild clematis flowers

green woodpeckers

Wildlife mission for children

Butterfly watch. How close can you get to a butterfly? Move slowly and silently and keep your shadow away from the butterfly. Can you see all the colours on its wings?

Distance:

About 3 miles (5 km). Allow 2 hours.

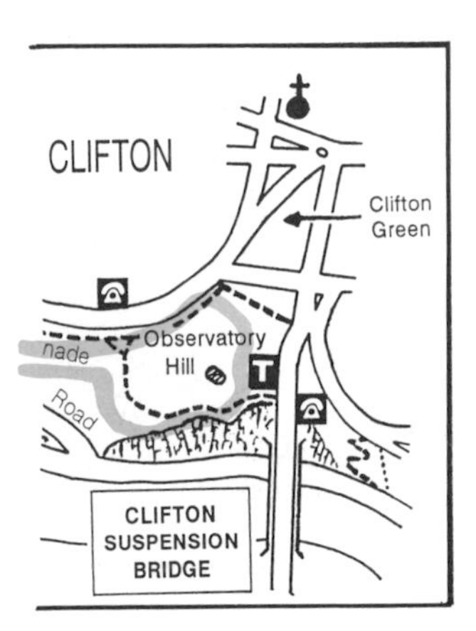

MAP KEY

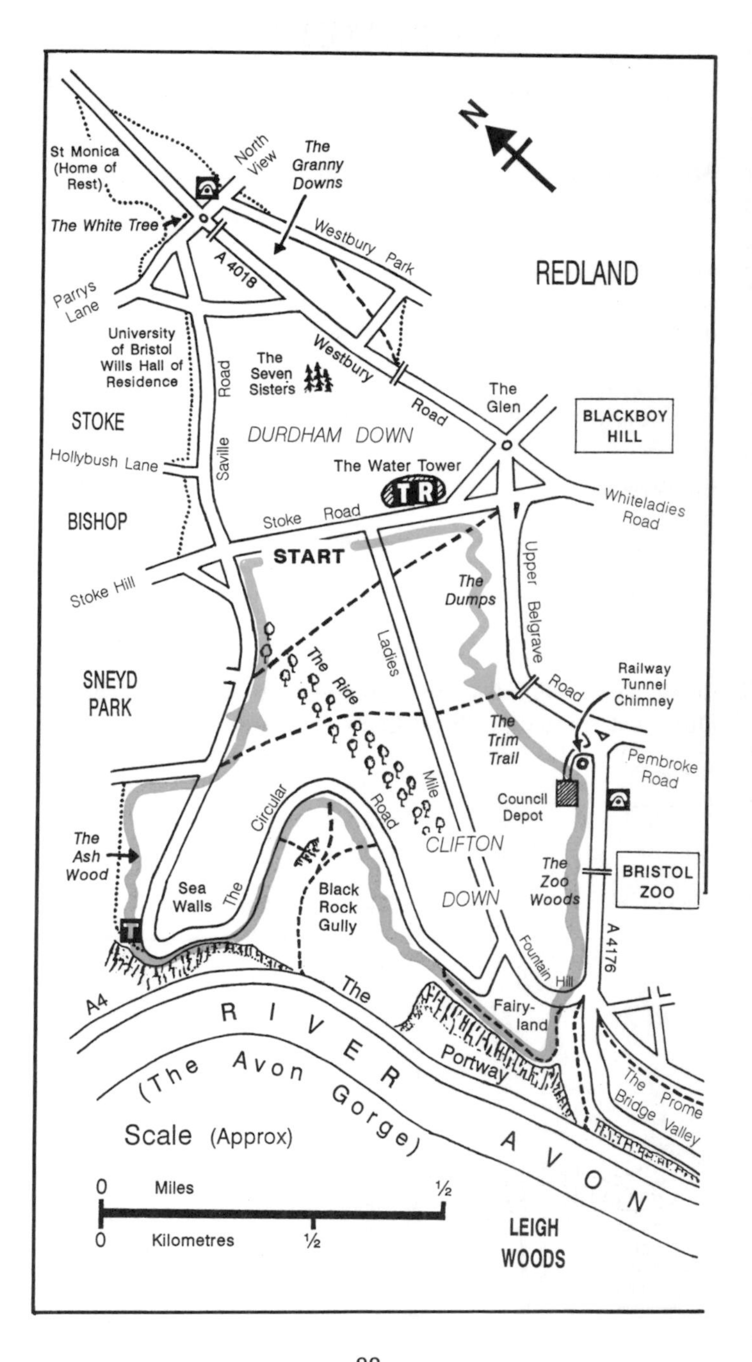

N
St Monica (Home of Rest)
North View
The Granny Downs
The White Tree
Westbury Park
REDLAND
A 4018
Parrys Lane
University of Bristol Wills Hall of Residence
The Seven Sisters
Westbury Road
The Glen
BLACKBOY HILL
STOKE
Saville Road
DURDHAM DOWN
Hollybush Lane
The Water Tower
TR
Whiteladies Road
BISHOP
Stoke Road
START
Stoke Hill
The Dumps
Upper Belgrave Road
The Ride
Ladies Mile
SNEYD PARK
Railway Tunnel Chimney
The Trim Trail
Pembroke Road
Council Depot
The Ash Wood
The Circular Road
CLIFTON DOWN
BRISTOL ZOO
The Zoo Woods
Sea Walls
Black Rock Gully
T
A 4176
Fountain Hill
A4
The Portway
Fairy-land
RIVER AVON
(The Avon Gorge)
The Bridge Valley Prome
Scale (Approx)
0 Miles ½
0 Kilometres ½
LEIGH WOODS

SEPTEMBER

The Blackberry Walk

An intriguing walk through autumn's richness.

Look out for:

blackberries
hawthorn berries
elderberries

conkers*
harebells
tormentil

goldfinches
robins (singing again)

garden cross spiders

squirrels

* conkers: these can be ready for gathering at any time during September and October. If they are 'early' see the October walk.

Wildlife mission for children

Berry watch. How many different berries can you spot? Don't eat them unless you know they are blackberries.

Distance:

About 3 miles (5 km). Allow 2 hours.

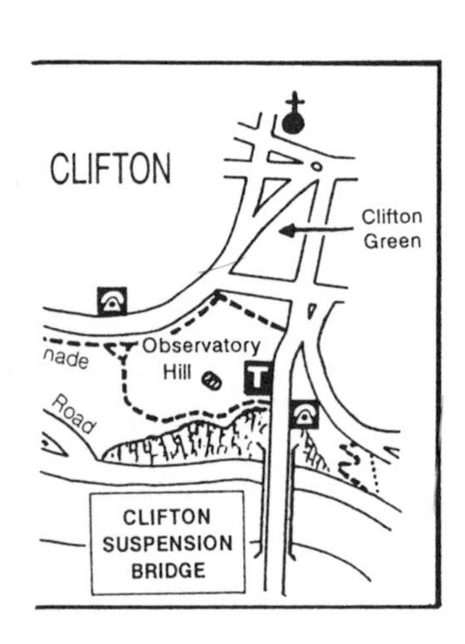

MAP KEY

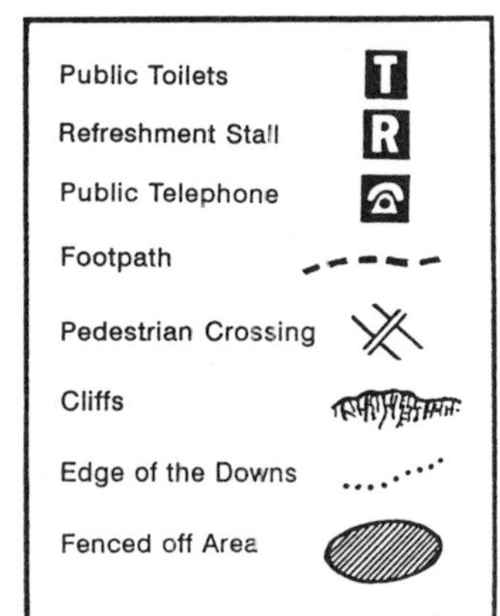

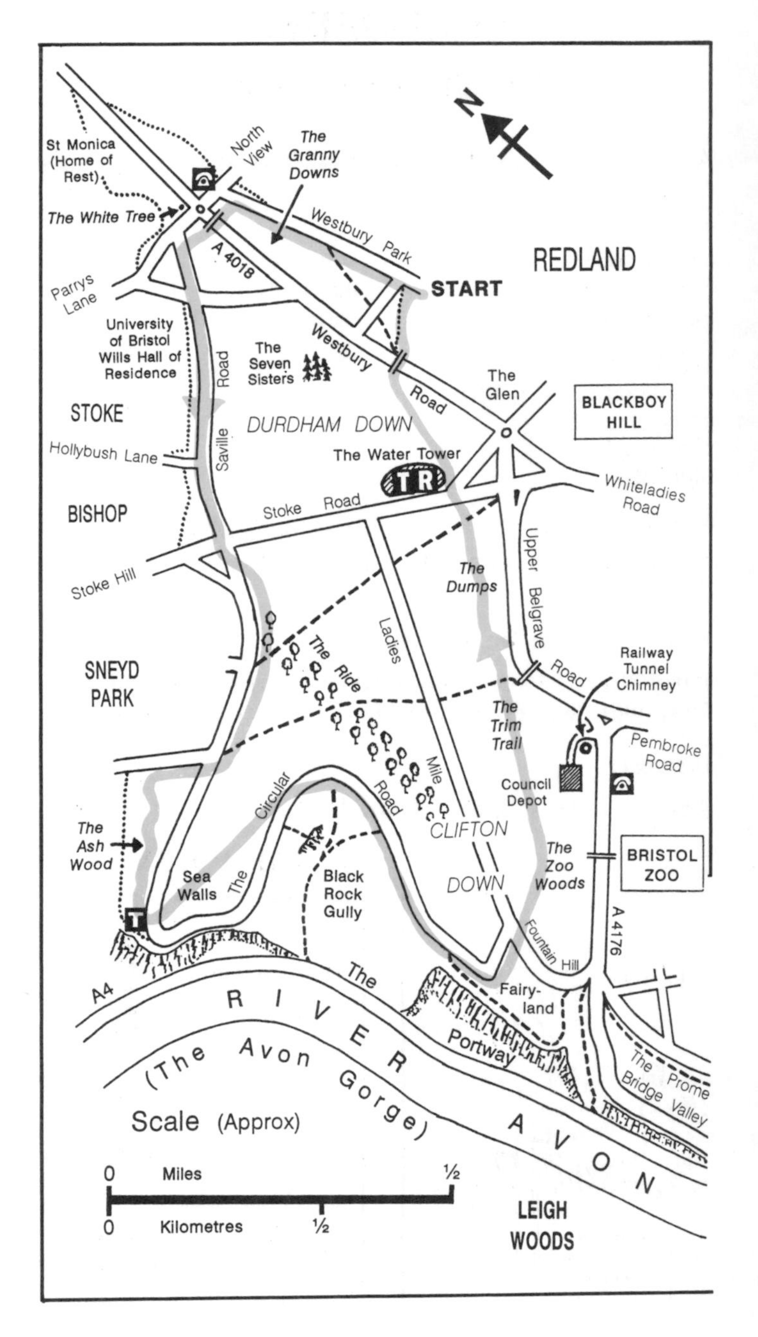
St Monica (Home of Rest)
North View
The Granny Downs
The White Tree
Westbury Park
A 4018
REDLAND
START
Parrys Lane
University of Bristol Wills Hall of Residence
The Seven Sisters
Westbury Road
The Glen
BLACKBOY HILL
STOKE
Saville Road
DURDHAM DOWN
Hollybush Lane
The Water Tower
TR
Whiteladies Road
BISHOP
Stoke Road
Stoke Hill
Upper Belgrave Road
The Dumps
Ladies Mile
The Ride
SNEYD PARK
Railway Tunnel Chimney
The Trim Trail
Pembroke Road
Council Depot
Circular Road
CLIFTON DOWN
The Ash Wood
The Zoo Woods
BRISTOL ZOO
Sea Walls
The
Black Rock Gully
A 4176
Fountain Hill
T
The Portway
Fairy-land
A4
RIVER AVON
(The Avon Gorge)
The Bridge Valley
Prome
Scale (Approx)
0 Miles ½
0 Kilometres ½
LEIGH WOODS

OCTOBER

The Conker Walk

A walk through the famous conker harvest but don't miss the fungi.

Look out for:

conkers
ivy flowers
clematis plumes (old man's beard)
earthball fungi
shaggy parasol fungi
amethyst deceiver fungi

green woodpeckers
pied wagtails
blue tits

autumn leaves – especially lime, maple, silver birch, elm

Wildlife mission for children

Look out for a 'small world'. Can you find a tiny patch of land with lots in it – acorns, fungi, leaves, conkers, perhaps a feather. When you get home, see if you can remember everything in your 'small world'.

Distance:

About 3½ miles (6 km). Allow 2¼ hours.

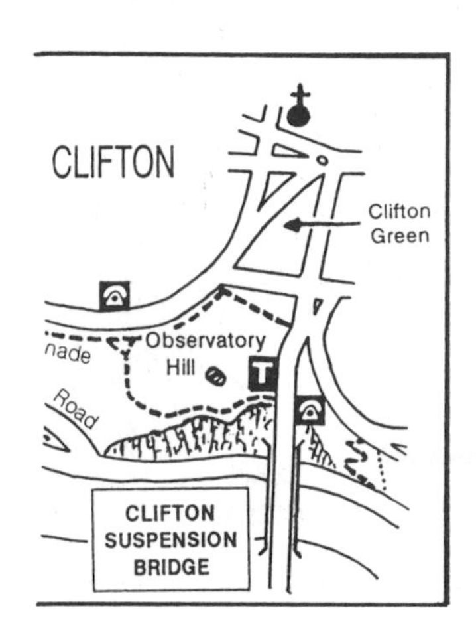

MAP KEY

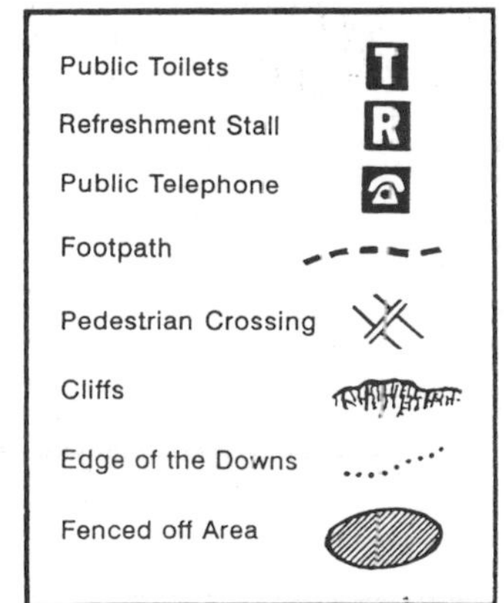

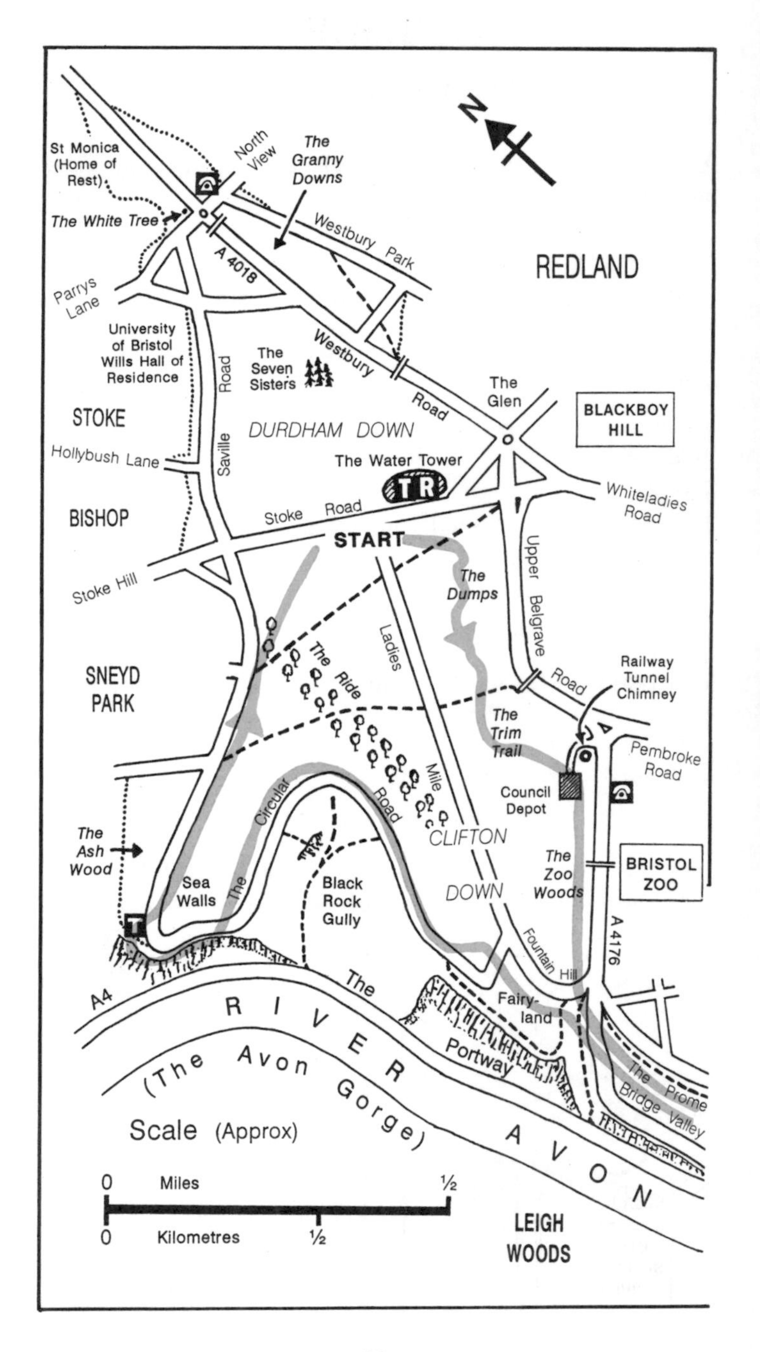
St Monica (Home of Rest)
North View
The Granny Downs
The White Tree
Westbury Park
A 4018
REDLAND
Parrys Lane
University of Bristol Wills Hall of Residence
The Seven Sisters
Westbury Road
The Glen
BLACKBOY HILL
STOKE
DURDHAM DOWN
Saville Road
Hollybush Lane
The Water Tower
Whiteladies Road
BISHOP
Stoke Road
START
Stoke Hill
The Dumps
Upper Belgrave Road
Ladies Mile Road
The Ride
SNEYD PARK
Railway Tunnel Chimney
The Trim Trail
Pembroke Road
Council Depot
The Circular Road
CLIFTON DOWN
The Ash Wood
The Zoo Woods
BRISTOL ZOO
Sea Walls
Black Rock Gully
Fountain Hill
A 4176
A4
The Portway
Fairy-land
RIVER AVON
(The Avon Gorge)
The Bridge Valley
The Prome
Scale (Approx)
0 Miles ½
0 Kilometres ½
LEIGH WOODS

NOVEMBER

The Autumn Leaves Walk

A rewarding time for a long walk. Choose one of those mellow, sunny days to see the Avon Gorge in its full glory.

Look out for:

autumn leaves, especially beech, silver birch, horse chestnut, elm, ash, lime
look over to Leigh Woods for the autumn colours
acorns
spindle berries

fungi including jew's ear fungus (look on elder)

magpies
bullfinches
long-tailed tits
pied wagtails

Wildlife mission for children

Wind watch. Which birds seem to enjoy flying in high winds?

Distance:

About 4¼ miles (7 km). Allow 2¾ hours.

MAP KEY

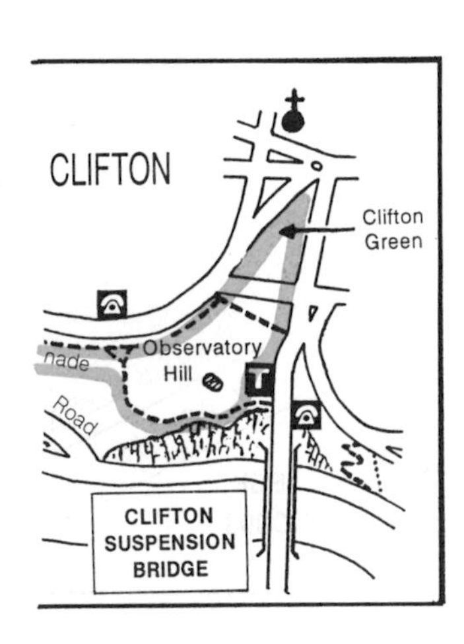

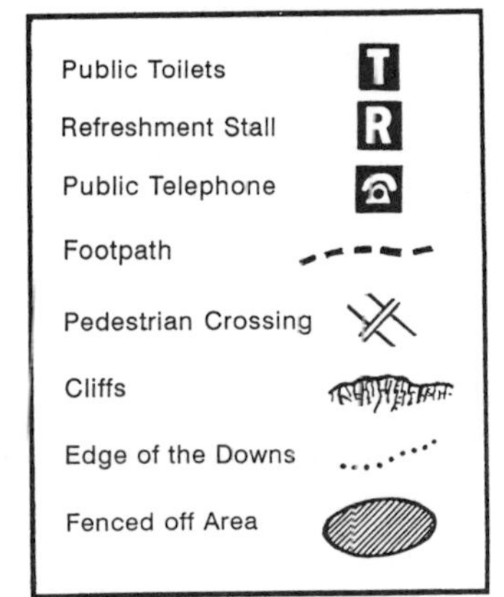

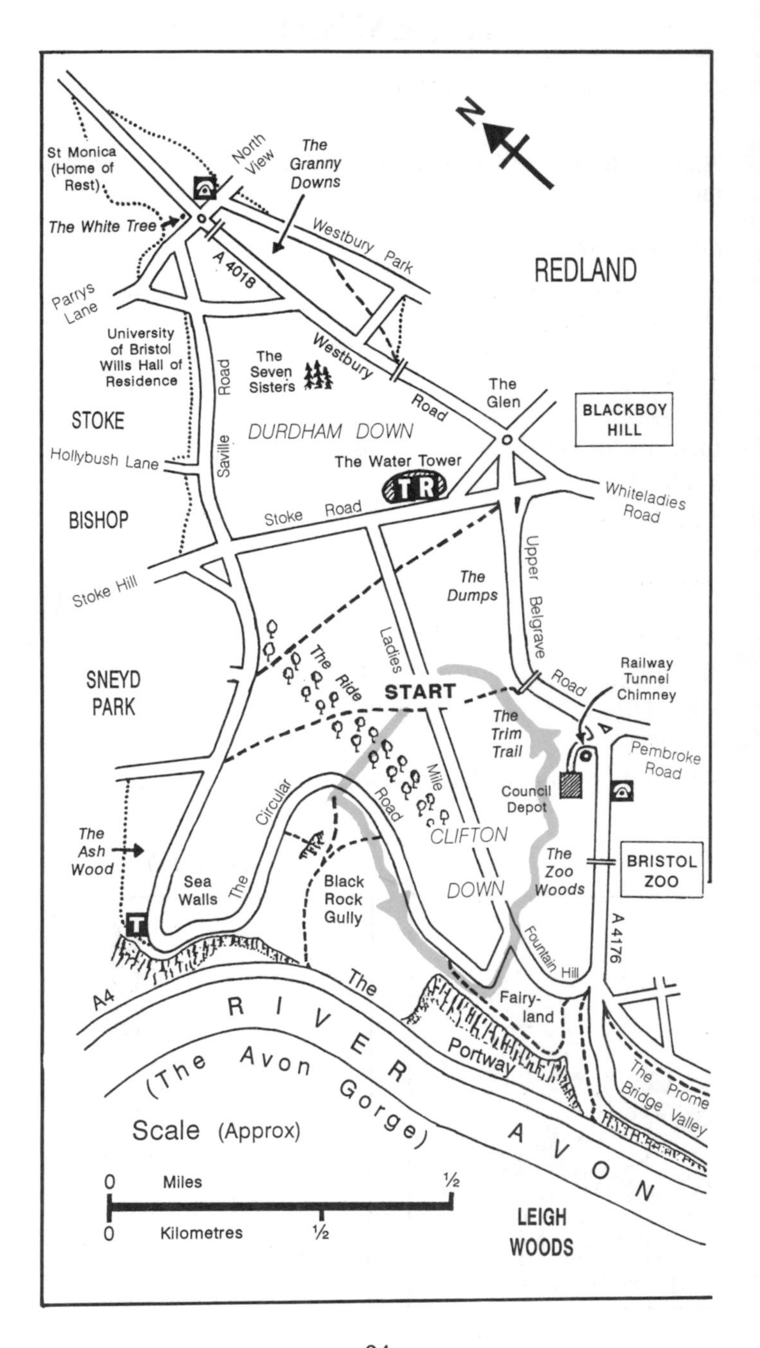

N
St Monica
(Home of
Rest)
North
View
The
Granny
Downs
The White Tree
Westbury Park
A 4018
REDLAND
Parrys
Lane
University
of Bristol
Wills Hall of
Residence
The
Seven
Sisters
Westbury
Road
The
Glen
BLACKBOY
HILL
STOKE
Saville
Road
DURDHAM DOWN
Hollybush Lane
The Water Tower
TR
Whiteladies
Road
BISHOP
Stoke Road
Stoke Hill
Upper Belgrave Road
The
Dumps
The Ride
Ladies Mile
SNEYD
PARK
START
Railway
Tunnel
Chimney
The
Trim
Trail
Pembroke
Road
Council
Depot
The Circular Road
CLIFTON
DOWN
The
Ash
Wood
The
Zoo
Woods
BRISTOL
ZOO
Sea
Walls
Black
Rock
Gully
T
Fountain Hill
A 4176
A4
The Portway
Fairy-
land
RIVER AVON
(The Avon Gorge)
The Prome
Bridge Valley
Scale (Approx)
0 Miles ½
0 Kilometres ½
LEIGH
WOODS

DECEMBER

The Christmas Walk

Share your Christmas with a robin and look out for the mistletoe.

Look out for:

holly
ivy
mistletoe
yew berries
oak apples

herring gulls
blackbirds
blue tits
goldcrests
wrens
robins
pied wagtails

Wildlife mission for children

Robin watch. How many robins can you spot? Stay still in a fairly wooded area and see if a robin joins you.

Distance:

About 1¼ miles (2 km). Allow ¾ hour.

MAP KEY

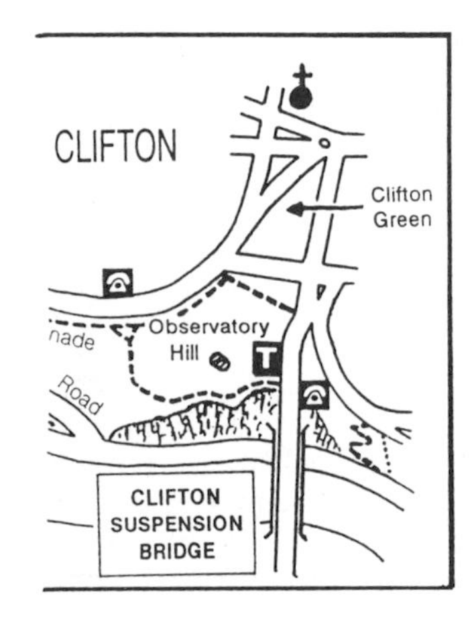

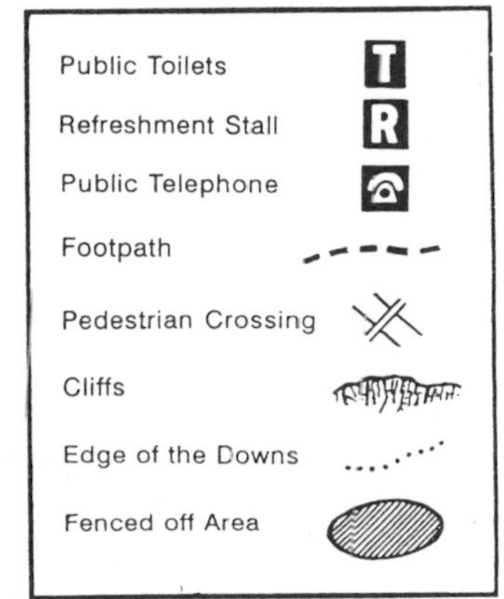

WATCHING WILDLIFE ON THE BRISTOL DOWNS

The Bristol Downs can be the wildlife nursery slopes for any enthusiast and observation skills learned here can be applied everywhere.

The essential activity is direct observation and this needs practice and information. The following suggestions will ensure that your observation is increasingly rewarding.

The birds of the Bristol Downs

Birds of the Downs are accustomed to people and many of them exhibit an unconcerned independence which is a great advantage to the observer. Robins sing from open perches; green woodpeckers sit on a bank beside a busy bus stop or feed close to family picnickers; jays visit areas near houses and kestrels appear to form relationships with regular visitors. It's obviously the duty and privilege of any Downs' birdwatcher to maintain the unthreatening atmosphere so that this situation may continue.

Moving closer

Although it's tricky when you're excited by the bird, animal or insect you've seen, make no sudden movements. Stop gently, watch and then move slowly, arms at your sides and if you are stalking an insect (especially a butterfly), don't let your shadow fall on it.

Variety

Variety is one key to developing expertise in observation. Vary your route (our walks will help), your pace of walking, the time of day and above all, vary the level at which you look.

Practise looking in levels. These five are the important levels:

ground level
herb (small plant) level
shrub level
tree level
the sky

For example, looking at different levels in May might produce a bumble-bee at ground level; cowslips and an orange tip butterfly at herb level; wayfaring blossom, a robin and a crab spider at shrub level; oak flowers, a treecreeper and long-tailed tits at tree level; swifts, starlings and a heron at sky level.

Our walks will encourage you to vary the terrain you cross and a mixture of open, bushy and wooded is usually the most rewarding. Remember to look into the Avon Gorge itself and across to Leigh Woods for the changing colours of the seasons there.

It's useful to build up a picture of the levels at which you may see certain birds. A green woodpecker, for example, a pied wagtail and a blackbird might all be seen on the ground, a goldfinch might be feeding on thistles (herb level), a wren might be in the undergrowth at shrub level, a willow warbler and mistle thrush might be at tree level and swifts in the sky. It's also helpful to know when migrant birds arrive and leave and which birds are with us all year round.

Eventually it becomes possible to listen in layers, too, and this includes the sound made by some insects.

Look again

Just as variety is one key to developing observation skills, so close and repeated attention to the same area is another key. Adopt an area you like and return to it, looking for the same birds and insects and watching the development of the plants and trees throughout the seasons.

All weathers

It's rewarding to observe in all weather conditions as this gives us a more complete picture of how wildlife behaves. After gales, too, it's possible to collect twigs, tree flowers, nests and small branches to take home and study in detail.

Reference books

A small library of wildlife reference books will become a necessity. A list of useful books is given on page 100.

WILDLIFE WATCHING WITH CHILDREN

Encouraging children to observe wildlife closely is itself a skill. I've found these approaches successful in both developing children's interests and skills and increasing my own effectiveness as a helpful adult.

Go with a mission
Missions can range from an expedition to discover if big birds have big calls and songs, to a ladybird hunt, a one-hour butterfly census and a squirrel safari. Suggestions for missions are included in our section on walks on the Downs.

I spy with my hawk-like eye
Can each member of the family spot an unusual wildlife detail? The olive-green sheen on a robin's back, the tiny red daisy in the grass, the long furry antenna on a shiny beetle.

Make a map
Adopt a small clump of the Downs (an area with bushes, trees and turf is best). Visit the area regularly. Have you attracted a robin? Help your children to make a map of the family clump and chart the flowers, trees, insects and birds you see there. It's interesting to study the stages of plant growth from cotyledon (first leaves growing from the seed) to seed production.

What size?
Take a ruler and compare sizes of flowers, leaves and fungi. Who can find the smallest buttercup, the largest mushroom?

Curiosity
Encourage your children to stop and look at whatever catches their eye. That sudden colour could be an unusual flower or a flower in an unusual place. That shuffling in the dead leaves is probably a blackbird – but it might be a weasel. Try to find out.

Wondering
It's important to wonder about wildlife for the fun of wondering as well as a boost to information-seeking back home. Wondering – even apparently impossible wondering – keeps curiosity and enthusiasm high. Wonderings shared are best of all:
I wonder how many colours there are on a butterfly's wing?

I wonder if trees sleep?
I wonder what the birds are saying?

Naming

Once interest is captured, learning the names of the wildlife on the Downs is a skill which develops quickly. However there are bound to be birds, flowers, trees and insects which are temporarily 'unknown' and it's useful to encourage children to give these a name of their own pending looking up the actual name. This fixes the main characteristics in the memory as well as giving personal appeal. For example, one family named yellow rattle 'golden rabbits' and another named jackdaws 'greyheads'.

Back home

Children often like to do something with their observations and this usually takes the form of a drawing or story.

It's interesting to make a museum of pine cones, fallen tree flowers, leaves, feathers, acorns and other objects gleaned from the ground.

Recording is the next step. This could be a simple nature diary, perhaps with a map of your adopted area.

Basic facts to record are:
the date
the weather
the time of day
what was seen
where it was seen
what it was doing.

Perhaps you could start a family nature newsletter!

RECOMMENDED READING

The AA Book of the British Countryside, (Drive Publications 1988).

Animals of Britain, (Reader's Digest 1984).

Birds of Britain, (Reader's Digest 1981).

M. Brooks & C. Knight, *A Complete Guide to British Butterflies*, (Cape 1982).

Michael Chinery, *Insects of Britain and Western Europe*, (Collins 1986).

Roger Phillips, *Mushrooms and other fungi of Great Britain and Europe*, (Pan 1981).

Trees and Shrubs, (Reader's Digest 1981).

Wild Flowers of Britain, (Reader's Digest 1981).

Roger Phillips, *Wild Flowers of Britain*, (Pan 1977).

R. Fitter, A. Fitter & M. Blamey, *The Wild Flowers of Britain and Northern Europe*, (Collins 1985).

Heather & Robin Tanner, *Woodland Plants*, (Impact Books 1987).

The Wildlife of the Avon Gorge

The Avon Gorge, (Bristol Naturalists' Society, Special Issue 1, 1989).

Averil Morley, *Bird Life on Clifton Downs*, (undated – 1934 or 1935. Bristol Central Library, Local Studies Class number L 59.30337).

Bristol's Urban Ecology, (Bristol Naturalists' Society, Special Issue 2, 1991).

Geraldine Taylor, *Planting Acorns; An Adventure Story & Guidebook – How to give your City Child a Country Childhood*, (Impact Books 1986).

Eye on Local Nature Magazine, quarterly by post from 28 Berkeley Road, Westbury Park, Bristol BS6 7PJ.
(This magazine focuses upon the Downs and the Avon Gorge, with contributions from Bristol and elsewhere).

WILDLIFE ORGANISATIONS

Avon Wildlife Trust,
Bristol Wildlife Centre,
Jacobs Wells Road,
Bristol BS8 1DR

The Royal Society for the Protection of Birds (RSPB),
The Lodge,
Sandy,
Bedfordshire SG19 2DL

The Bristol Naturalists' Society,
The Hon. Treasurer, Philip Nethercott,
6 Hazelwood Road, Hazelwood Court,
Bristol BS9 1PU

The Friends of the Bristol Downs,
28 Berkeley Road,
Westbury Park,
Bristol BS6 7PJ

THE AUTHORS

Geraldine Taylor is an author and journalist, specialising in education and natural history. Her book, *Planting Acorns: An Adventure Story and Guidebook – How to Give Your City Child a Country Childhood* (Impact Books) tells the story of her family's involvement with Bristol wildlife. Geraldine Taylor writes for national magazines and broadcasts, often on wildlife. She is editor of *Eye on Local Nature Magazine* and a Voluntary Warden with English Nature.

Keith Taylor is a nature photographer and popular local lecturer on the wild flowers of the Avon Gorge, specialising in orchid photography. Keith Taylor is a Voluntary Warden with English Nature and a member of the team who look after the Avon Gorge National Nature Reserve. He is publisher of *Eye on Local Nature Magazine.*

Susanna Kendall is an illustrator who lives in the Bristol area. Her recent work has included writing and illustrating two children's picture books, *Will You play with Me?* and *I Could Be . . .* both published by Collins and, working with author Penny Speller, illustrating *Princess Emerald* for Oxford University Press. The present drawings for the *Secret Bristol Downs* are her first natural history illustrations.

Peter Taylor, the editor, founded *Eye on Local Nature Magazine*, and is currently reading English at the University of Leeds.

INDEX

YOUR OWN NATURE NOTES

YOUR OWN NATURE NOTES

YOUR OWN NATURE NOTES

YOUR OWN NATURE NOTES

YOUR OWN NATURE NOTES